# THE
# KESWICK
# STORY

Also by John Pollock

JAMES BELMOUR

# THE KESWICK STORY

## The Authorized History
## of the Keswick Convention – Updated!

### REV. DR. JOHN CHARLES POLLOCK
### with IAN RANDALL

CLC PUBLICATIONS

Fort Washington, PA 19034

*Published by CLC Publications*

*U.S.A.*
P.O. Box 1449, Fort Washington, PA 19034

*GREAT BRITAIN*
51 The Dean, Alresford, Hants. SO24 9BJ

*AUSTRALIA*
P.O. Box 213, Bungalow, Cairns, QLD 4870

*NEW ZEALAND*
10 MacArthur Street, Feilding

*ISBN 0-87508-582-2*

# Contents

# Preface

When I was invited by the Keswick Convention Council to write the history of the Convention, I accepted as an honor and a duty.

In the stories of some Christian lives and movements, the closer you get to their unadorned, private selves, the less attractive you find them. With Keswick it has been the reverse. The deeper I dug into the original materials, the nearer I got to the character of the men who founded and developed Keswick, the more profound grew my realization that here was something used mightily, not despite its principles but only when truly loyal to them. Respect changed to conviction. Interest became commitment.

I am delighted therefore that this book, first published in 1964, is being republished forty years on. Keswick continues to flourish and expand, and its more recent history has been admirably told in the millenium convention book, *Transforming Keswick* by Ian Randall and Charles Price. I am grateful to Ian Randall for kindly providing a perceptive summary for this edition. I am very grateful to Mr. Peter Maiden, chairman, for his Foreword and would also like to thank Mr. David Bradley, general director and Mr. Maurice L. Rowlandson, who was general secretary for fifteen years, for their help.

But the origins of the Keswick Convention and its first eighty years stand on their own as a remarkable episode in Christian history. The story will, I believe, be as inspiring to a wide new readership as it was to me as I researched and wrote, all those years ago.

*John C. Pollock*

# Foreword

We are very encouraged to see this reprint of *The Keswick Story* by John Pollock.

Those of us who have responsibility for the Convention today and its associated ministries must never forget this remarkable history.

From its founding in 1875 in a small town in the British province of Cumbria, a national and indeed international impact has been made through the preaching of the Word of God. As you read this history, I'm sure you'll agree that this has truly been "a work of God."

There have been many changes in the Convention over the years and the pace of change has certainly increased in the last twenty years. But certain things remain, and must remain, constant. "Keswick" must continue to commit to the proclamation of the Lordship of Christ through the exposition of the Word of God. The call to a life of practical holiness in the light of His sovereignty must continue to be heard. The obvious response to this in Christian unity, evangelism, and mission must never be neglected.

I was inspired again by reading this excellently written history.

On behalf of the Keswick Council,
Peter Maiden, Chairman
2006

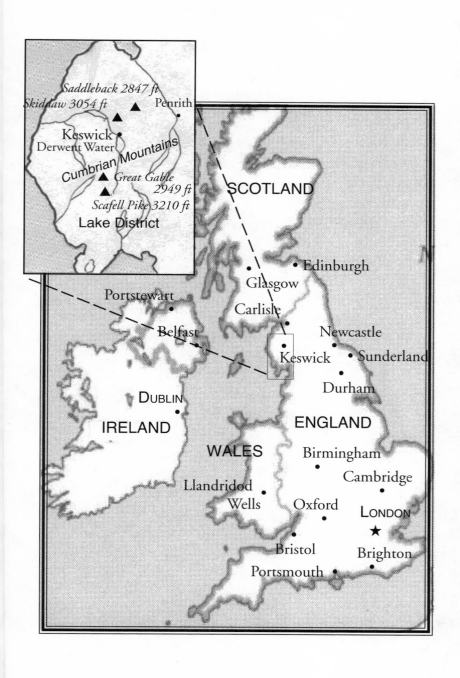

# One

## The American

On a perfect June morning of 1875 the Vicar of St. John's, the Anglican church in Keswick, stood at his study window gazing at one of the finest views in England.

Derwent Water lay masked by outlying houses of the town, by meadows and hedgerows. But on either side of the lake, the hills—green with young grass and mottled by clumps of trees—converged on the Cumbrian range beyond Borrowdale, an amphitheater of Lakeland summits: Glaramara and Great Gable, and Scafell Pike behind, softened by heat haze under a blue sky.

Canon Dundas Harford-Battersby, tall and slight in black clerical dress and white stock, his face clean shaven, hair already turning silver although he was only fifty-two, hands slender and sensitive, turned to a scene closer at hand. His eye lit up. White canvas billowed in the field at the bottom of the parsonage garden as workmen tugged and pulled to erect a great tent to seat nearly a thousand. All would be ready for the three days' Convention to start early next week on June 29th.

The parlormaid entered, carrying a telegram on a silver salver. The Canon slit it open. He gasped. In blunt telegraphic terms the intended chairman and chief speaker of the Convention, Robert Pearsall Smith, declared that his health had collapsed and that instead of visiting Keswick he and his wife would return immediately to America. The Convention had been arranged around the Pearsall Smiths—he to preach, she to expound the Bible in her inimitable manner.

The tail end of a week gave too short notice for Harford-Battersby to summon substitutes, and besides, he had been attacked enough for announcing the meetings, by important men whose opinion he valued: this telegram must be a providential warning that they were right. He would cancel. Then he paused. His mind flew back to an evening nine months before, when "I got," he described it subsequently, "a revelation of Christ to my soul so extraordinary, so glorious and precious that from that day it illuminated my life. I found *He* was *all* I wanted. . . . Whenever I have trusted Him with a full and entire trust I have found Him all I needed."

In the words of his son, "My father spread the telegraphic message before the Lord." He arose, wrote a note, and tugged the bell rope. He told the parlormaid to have the groom ride at once over the Whinlatter Pass to Mr. Robert Wilson at Broughton Grange.

Harford-Battersby looked again at the steadfast, peaceful hills, no work of man but of God.

—— —— —— —— ——

The story had begun more than two years earlier, in London.

The spring of 1873 brought across from Philadelphia a glass manufacturer of forty-six, Robert Pearsall Smith. "He is full of fun and spirits but wonderfully interesting and edifying spiritually," the young daughter of one of his hosts described him in her diary, "filling the house with sunshine. . . . He is such a dear man and has such a lovely restful expression." Smith suffered frequent acute headaches, but the American's courtesy and graciousness under pain merely emphasized what he had come to impart.

He found Evangelicalism dominant in much of Great Britain, yet slowly suffocating in an atmosphere of introspection and gloom. It seemed to be a world of crepe and wails, and preoccupation with death; of people who were disconcerted by sanctions and inhibitions. Fervent Christians groaned, and gloried, in unceasing inner conflict. Many were afraid to be happy: happiness was being sapped by their lurking sense of guilt. The mass of ordinary church- and chapel-goers kept their religious and secular selves in separate compartments, wearing now one, now the other as different dresses of the personality. Moreover, England in the early 1870s was veering into bitter controversies: evangelicals were wrangling with Oxford Movement men, yet both were allied uneasily against liberals and agnostic scientists. Meanwhile, relations between churchmen and dissenters, with a few honorable exceptions, remained frigid.

Only against this background of conflict, personal and national, can the impact of Pearsall Smith be understood.

He wanted to share a secret, a secret which had always been a segment of the Christian heritage. As a London clergyman who supported Smith would often proclaim, "It is not new, though it may be new to you. Holy men of God of all ages have yearned after victory over daily sin, and found it in the Indwelling of the Victor." The Wesleys in their teaching and their hymns were full of it, as Methodism had never forgotten. More lately the annual Conference founded by William Pennefather of St. Jude's, Mildmay, North London, and its Scottish counterpart at Perth, had among their aims "the promotion of personal holiness" and the "desire to bring into closer social communion the members of various churches." But Pennefather, who had radiated a happy, infectious faith, had recently died. The Revival of 1859 had created widespread spiritual yearning, increased during the sixties by a book from America called *The Higher Christian Life*, written by an itinerant Presbyterian minister, William Edwin Boardman. Trained theologians could tear its argument to shreds; detractors grumbled about "enough error to poison a parish." Yet it possessed a rugged power to influence for good tens of thousands on both sides of the Atlantic.

The catalyst, however, effecting a lasting change in English religion was the arrival in 1873 of Robert Pearsall Smith, followed a year later by his accomplished wife, Hannah Whitall Smith. That two such people should have been cast for vital, if brief, roles remains an inscrutable mystery of Providence.

Both were of Quaker extraction, and Hannah had a Quaker stillness about her and often used the distinctive Quaker "thee," but they cared nothing about denominational labels. They had made a great discovery: "that it was really a fact that the Lord was both able and willing to deliver us out of every temptation if we would but trust Him to do it. . . . It seemed to me," Hannah wrote, "such an amazing and delightful thing that I could not keep it to myself." She called it "the Christian's secret of a happy life."

The Pearsall Smiths traveled around the eastern states of America, Hannah proving a gracious and adept Bible teacher and her husband a persuasive speaker and chairman. Their charm, happiness, and evident genuineness encouraged the discerning to overlook the dangerous remarks that both dropped occasionally. "I never gave Smith credit for much intelligence," wrote an English friend; "It was his heart, not his head, which attracted me." Hannah had her own pet heresy: she believed that all, however impenitent in this life, would in the fullness of eternity reach Heaven.

The exertion of running the Whitall glass works in Pennsylvania while in such demand as a speaker eventually cracked Pearsall Smith's health. It had not been robust since a riding accident long before, which had prostrated him for two years with congestion of the brain and left a legacy of headaches. In the spring of 1873 he took sick leave in Europe, Hannah staying at home with the children.

He carried letters of introduction and soon was meeting Anglican clergymen and Nonconformist ministers, politicians and other influential laymen at private breakfasts, the meal for intimate discussions in that leisured age, and other informal gatherings. On Thursday, May 1, at the Curzon Street Chapel in Mayfair, London, he addressed a group of fifteen or sixteen. One of them was a thirty-five-year-old vicar from Richmond in Surrey, southwest of London.

Evan Hopkins had been trained as a mining engineer, but at the age of twenty the remark of a gnarled coastguardsman on the Dorset coast, "I have served the devil for forty years but I mean now to serve the Lord Jesus Christ," had set him on the path to ordination. Black-haired, with square-cut face framed with black side whiskers, the vigorous Vicar of the new parish of Holy Trinity, Richmond, had never regretted his vocation. But he had found, when a slum curate in London's dockland, and then in the West End, and now building a congregation in a church gleaming with new neogothic stone and smelling strongly of varnish, that militant evangelical preaching and visiting were exhausting, plodding, uphill tasks. He listened eagerly to Pearsall Smith's exciting message.

Evan Hopkins returned to Richmond. His wife saw at once that he was "deeply moved by what he had heard and experienced. He told me he was like one looking out on a land wide and beautiful, flowing with milk and honey. It was to be possessed. *It was his.* As he described it all I felt that he had received an overflowing blessing far beyond anything I knew."

After dinner and a good-night peep at fourteen-month-old Evan and the twins born only six weeks before, they sat up late with their Bibles. "Pearsall Smith took that verse in 2 Corinthians, 'God is able to make all grace abound towards you,'" Hopkins said as he tried to explain what had happened. "I see I've all along been making that verse read, 'God is able to make *some* grace abound towards you, that ye sometimes, having some sufficiency, in *some* things, may abound to some good works.' But look at it! *God is able!* It's all, all, all—five *all*s. He is *always* able, to make *all* grace abound, there is no lack, no cessation of the abundant supply—in *all* things—heart needs, trials, Christian service. It is not merely that the Lord will help me. It's that He will do *all*, and will live in me His own holy life, the only holiness possible to us."

They talked on and on. At first, Isabella recalls, "It seemed as if a gulf had come between us. . . . Oh, I was hungry. At last, quite simply, but very really, I too took God at His word and accepted Christ as my indwelling Lord and Life, and believed that He did enthrone Himself in my heart."

Evan Hopkins, with his scientist's mind, set out to analyze what he called his "May Day" experience. The parishoners were not left long in doubt. The parson and his wife had a new ebullience, assurance, unflagging zest, and above all, contagious joy.

———— ·—— ·—— ·————

Pearsall Smith traveled widely in southern England to address conferences expressly convened by clergy and ministers. Through these, and his writings and Hannah's, scores of men and women found the "Christian's secret of a happy life," or, in the rather unfortunate phrase which gained circulation, "the blessing." The movement stirred little as yet beyond the upper classes. Besetting sins to be overcome were a tattling tongue, angry looks, viciousness on the croquet lawn, impatience with servants ("Does the sudden pull of the bell ever give notice in the kitchen that a good temper has been lost by the head of the household?"). Women discovered inner strength under days of "feeling poorly," men ceased to worry about the next bank failure, parents knew peace when death struck the nursery.

Several well-known Christians acknowledged a new quality in their living, and before 1873 was over Frances Ridley Havergal, already famous for her hymns and devotional verses, "saw clearly the blessedness of true consecration. I saw it as a flash of electric light . . . so I just utterly yielded myself to Him, and utterly trusted Him to keep me." And thus she was able before her early death to write those hymns indelibly identified with Keswick: *Like a River Glorious* and *Take My Life and Let It Be.*

Other notable Christians were disturbed or angered.

Prominent clergy were convinced that Pearsall Smith taught Sinless Perfection. Outraged letters appeared in the *Record,* the thrice-weekly organ of Church evangelicals. Editorials and articles mauled "Pearsall Smithism." Far away in Cumberland, Canon Harford-Battersby read Smith's books. He scented danger, but when the *Record* printed a thoroughly unfair review of Smith's book *Holiness by Faith,* "I could not help writing off my thoughts about it on the spur of the moment."

While he worked in Keswick and went for a holiday in Scotland, Harford-Battersby worried. "I am feeling much inward struggle and questioning about this 'higher Christian life' which is so much talked of and written about," he wrote in his diary. Reading Pearsall Smith and Hannah had "made me utterly dissatisfied with myself and my state. I feel that I am dishonoring God and am wretched myself by living as I do. . . . God reveal to me the secret of this 'more excellent way' and enable me to walk in it now and always. Amen."

When Harford-Battersby made that diary entry in September 1873, Pearsall Smith, Evan Hopkins, three other men and four women were away in the Alps near Chamonix below Mont Blanc, happily making expeditions or enjoying Bible studies and hymn singing, "ten days spent in waiting upon God—generally three meetings a day—often in the wood on the mountainside."

Several of the party, as they met regularly at Keswick in afteryears, would say that the first real Keswick had been held in the Alps.

# Two

---

# A Park in Hampshire

The year 1874 was when the Moody and Sankey revival became a factor of national importance in Britain—without which the "Higher Life" movement might have fizzled out.

The burly, genial D. L. Moody, a New Englander in his mid-thirties, of powerful voice and rapid ungrammatical speech, bouncy humor, sensitive understanding of human problems and unshakable faith in the love of God, had begun casually in York in the summer of 1873 with his handsome young singer, Ira D. Sankey. The Americans passed farther north to Sunderland and Newcastle in the autumn, still almost unknown, and not until the astonishing Edinburgh campaign at the turn of the year, followed by months in Glasgow, did Moody and Sankey become internationally famous. They worked in Scotland and Ireland through most of 1874, but were the talk of the British Isles; on return to England in November they swept triumphantly from city to city, moving all classes, from the destitute to duchesses, reaching the climax of the great London campaign of March to July 1875.

What Pearsall Smith taught, Moody had learned for himself. After some ten years of high-charged, breakneck mission service in the Chicago slums and at the battlefronts of the Civil War, there came a period of "great hunger in my soul," of opposition to the will of God, of craving "that God would fill me with His Holy Spirit." It had brought him, shortly after the Chicago Fire of 1871, to complete surrender, followed by "such an experience of His love that I had to ask Him to stay His hand." Moody therefore understood and sympathized with Pearsall Smith. But he mistrusted the divisions Smith caused which contrasted with the broad measure of support undergirding Sankey and himself. Moody wrote to an American friend who was coming over: "I do not think you had better get in with any clique—Smith has a party, but he does not carry the church with him, and I find it is better to keep free to do one thing, to preach the simple gospel."*

Moody and Sankey were the essential background to the next events.

Pearsall Smith was invited to meet dons and other senior members of Cambridge University. In May 1874 he returned for several days with undergraduates, in the course of which he mentioned the American summer custom of camp meetings, when Christians would "go out into the woods for a week or ten days, and seek together in long breaths to draw in the influx of the Spirit. The result has been wonderful." The

---

* For "clique" Moody actually wrote "click." He could not spell and never punctuated (the dash and commas are inserted). For his story, see my *Moody without Sankey* (Hodder and Stoughton, 1963); the current edition (2005) is by Christian Focus.

Cambridge men said they wished they could do that too.

Hannah Whitall Smith had now joined her husband. She took London society by storm. "She was tall, fair," a contemporary described her, "with clear-cut features, and well-opened dark blue eyes." She had "light, active movements and glad, animated expression . . . and in her speech there was a freshness, directness, and force of expression, with singular facility of illustration, that were very captivating." Hannah became intimate with Georgina Cowper-Temple, wife of a prominent Member of Parliament who had inherited Broadlands Park in Hampshire from his stepfather, the jaunty old pagan Prime Minister, Lord Palmerston. One day Mrs. Smith happened to refer to the Cambridge undergraduates' desire for a camp meeting. Cowper-Temple impulsively offered Broadlands.

William Cowper-Temple (afterwards Lord Mount Temple), who has gone into English history as author of the Cowper-Temple clause in the Education Act of 1870, which ensured unsectarian Bible teaching in the new state schools, was a model landowner, a philanthropist, a strong—if unconventional—Christian, and of serene sweet-tempered disposition: "All about him seemed perfect peace." He was at home in both ballroom and prayer meeting, a teetotaller and ardent temperance advocate who numbered his friends among all political parties and churches, and was incurably inquisitive, being one of the earliest dabblers in spiritualism.

Having offered Broadlands, he planned to provide tents for the Cambridge men and to invite a choice selection of guests to the mansion for a small informal conference. The Pearsall Smiths scattered invitations widely. "A *very* small meeting could hardly be a success, even to those attending,"

Smith wrote to Cowper-Temple on June 8th from Paris, where he was preaching by interpretation. Hannah told Mrs. Cowper-Temple how it should be arranged, in words that might well describe the intention behind all similar gatherings: "In the first place, in order for it to be a successful conference, the call to it must be very *definite*. It has been proved a thousand times that meetings held expressly for the definite purpose of the promotion of holiness or the Higher Christian Life are infinitely more blessed than even the same people meeting indefinitely. The very fact of receiving such an invitation as I would suggest will make people think on the subject, and will bring them, if they come, in a much more *prepared* state of mind."

The Broadlands Conference assembled on July 17th. The hundred or so men and women who stayed a week as the Cowper-Temples' guests (many more came for the Sunday afternoon) reflected their hosts' catholic tastes: Nonconformist bankers jostled with ritualistic curates, peers with parsons, novelists with temperance reformers. They overflowed into farmhouses on the estate and the inns of Romsey, and filled the Georgian mansion to the attics, while Oxford and Cambridge undergraduates had their camp in the park. All ate together in the large oak-paneled dining room under Romney's "Lady Hamilton" and a Tintoretto and a Giorgione.

Most of the meetings were out of doors. The success of the Conference largely depended on its setting, away from the rush of towns. "A more suitable place it would not be possible to find," Evan Hopkins thought. Another guest, Edna Jackson, recalled "the glorious beech trees under which we sat . . . the long stretches of the park, beyond which, in distance, were the beginnings of the New Forest, ...ver garden to the left, from which came the perfume ...agnolia and roses, and the sound of the fountain; behind us the lawn, bordered by cedars, elms and other trees, sloping to the river that made a music of its own."

The stated aim was to explore the Scriptural possibilities of faith as an unbroken walk with God and as "victory over all known sin." The weather was kind and days began with a seven o'clock prayer meeting under the trees in the "purity and freshness" of morning, and continued in informal conversational meetings presided over by Pearsall Smith and Bible Readings from Hannah. Cowper-Temple often led in extempore prayer, and much time was allowed for quiet, when groups wandered in the park, prayed under the trees or talked earnestly in pairs. "It did indeed seem as if one heart were shared by all," wrote the wife of the Recorder of London. "We seemed to ascend higher and higher and . . . to gather courage to make a fuller and more joyful consecration of body, soul and spirit to our Lord." "Christians too often meet only to *talk* about good and precious things: peace, joy, love and so on, but there we actually had the very things themselves" was the verdict of a pale little Frenchman, the dark-haired, dark-eyed Theodore Monod, a pastor in Paris and previously a lawyer in America, who had been profoundly influenced by Pearsall Smith in France. At Broadlands, on the last night, when he had taken his candle from the solemn looking butler and entered his room, Monod wrote the hymn by which he will always be remembered: *Oh, the Bitter Shame and Sorrow*, with its theme of the altered motto from the arrogant "All of self and none of Thee" through "Some of self . . . Less of self" to the declamation in the light of the Cross and the Saviour's abiding love: "None of self and all of Thee." It was set to music by a young Nonconformist minister, James Mountain, who already was becoming the composer of the movement.

A guest said: "We must repeat these meetings on a larger scale, when all who desire can attend." Another offered £500 to pay for a public conference, though in the event the money was not called upon.

Oxford, where the lodging houses would be empty during the university vacation, seemed an obvious, central location. The date was fixed for a bare five weeks ahead.

Canon Harford-Battersby, in Cumberland, read the open invitation to the Union Meeting for the Promotion of Scriptural Holiness at Oxford: "In every part of the country, the God of all grace has given to many of His children a feeling of deep dissatisfaction with their spiritual state." He could say *Amen* to that. The conveners of the Conference were sure Christian truth should and could influence character altogether beyond anything they had yet experienced. He assented, but mistrusted their assurance that they were not "reaching out towards new forms of doctrine or ecclesiastical system."

The Harford-Battersbys were on holiday at Silloth, a small resort on the Solway Firth with Lakeland rising behind and the Scottish hills across the water, and it happened that the parish church had mounted an evangelistic mission. The Vicar of Keswick, hating to be idle, offered to help the missioner, William Haslam, who himself had once been a High Churchman and was known as "the Parson converted by his own sermon."

The two men were not previously acquainted but the Canon soon discovered that bright old Haslam, a London incumbent, had long experienced the "higher Christian life." They talked round and round the subject while the younger Harford-Battersby children played on the sands. At last Haslam told Harford-Battersby that if he wanted really to understand, he should attend the imminent Oxford Conference.

Being an inquirer of crystal honesty, on holiday, and untroubled by the cost of a two hundred and fifty mile train journey, and never loath to revisit his beloved Oxford, Harford-Battersby on the spur of the moment decided to go.

# Three

## Grass in the High

Thomas Dundas Harford-Battersby had been bred to wealth and evangelical piety. His father, who was a younger son of Harford of Blaise Castle, and added the Battersby on inheriting property, was a banker in Bristol, and his mother had been a friend of Hannah More.*

From Harrow, Dundas went up to Balliol. After a brief fling with the fast set he swept into hero-worship of John Henry Newman, then Anglican Vicar of the University Church, and Archdeacon Manning, both to be Roman Cardinals, and in 1847 was ordained to a slum curacy in Gosport, counting himself a Tractarian or ritualist. He was introspective and tended to self-depreciation. He was high-souled and solemn. This was a time when earnest young men wore godliness openly in scarcely conscious pose: a fellow curate remembered Harford-Battersby's "lofty purity of look," and the future Archbishop Frederick Temple, a tutor

---

* His home for much of his boyhood, Stoke House near Clifton, became Clifton Theological College (now Trinity College, Bristol).

at Balliol, said, "He has the ten commandments written in his face." As a curate he labored faithfully, maintained rigorous self-examination and methodical devotion. He said afterwards that he was morbid, intellectually proud, and that "love did not enter my heart."

Grim realities of a slum parish sabotaged his loyalty to the Oxford Movement: "I wish that I had now again that simple faith with which I once received the gospel." By the summer of 1849 he could no longer work happily with his rector or fellow-curates, for "I believe Anglo-Catholicism to be inconsistent and untenable by an honest mind."

Had Harford-Battersby not once been Anglo-Catholic he never would have gone to Keswick.

In rethinking his doctrine he read a notable appraisal on church and ministry, *Catholic Thoughts* by Frederic Myers, Vicar of St. John's. Harford-Battersby wrote to Myers, and in autumn 1849, shortly after his twenty-seventh birthday, joined him as curate, but Myers—whose son F. W. H. Myers won fame as author of the oft-quoted epic poem *St. Paul* (now believed to have been mostly plagiarized from the Latin), and as a spiritualist and the first Englishman to swim Niagara—died in 1851. Hartford-Battersby was offered the living, which he retained until his death thirty-two years later. In 1854 he married a Scottish landowner's daughter, and that year, in his early thirties, he first identified himself publicly with the evangelicals.

Thus the founder of the Keswick Convention had not been cut to a mold. He did not become what he was by supine acceptance of surroundings. His was no shallow faith doctrinally, but the settled expression of an independent mind.

Harford-Battersby was greatly respected by the townsfolk and the neighboring "statesmen" of the dales as a painstaking preacher, pastor and evangelist. He showed sympathy towards Methodists and Plymouth Brethren (whereas at Gosport he had written "Dissent here is terrible"), and in 1858 began a united prayer meeting which led some years later to united activities, unusual in that day. Controversy saddened him, union delighted him. "His great idea was to get people together," said his sons.

Delicate of health, he was reserved and shy and nervous but had "a most musical and infectious laugh. His relations used to love to 'set him off laughing,' simply for the delight of hearing him." He was easily cast down and beset by lingering doubts and dissatisfaction. In 1860 Boardman's book moved him to exclaim, "Oh what a compound we are of good wishes and miserable performances! When, when shall it be otherwise? I do not realize the 'Higher Christian Life' which Dr. Boardman speaks of and which I have preached to others of—the life hid with Christ in God."

And now, fourteen years later, as he sat in the train through the Black Country and the Midlands nearing Oxford, the writings of Pearsall Smith and the persuasions of William Haslam had deepened his wistful longing for spiritual power.

---

Oxford, in a long vacation, lapsed into quiet except for the chimes above the mild commerce of a county town, for this was forty years before the rise of the motor industry.

Grass was said to grow in the High.

When Harford-Battersby alighted in sight of the towers and spires on Saturday, August 29, 1874, he found the city filling with visitors, nine hundred or more (the sponsors claimed between a thousand and twelve hundred). A "striking feature was the presence of so many middle-aged and elderly clergymen and ministers," not fledglings of faith or callow tyros but veterans of service in slum and suburb and country, drawn by belief that the Conference might renew vision, or that its claims at least should be investigated. A number of Continental pastors had crossed the Channel, including Germans and French, who, at Oxford, were able to bury bitter enmity a mere year after the last German troops had withdrawn from all invaded provinces except Alsace and Lorraine. He went to the Clarendon Hotel, which offered a special price of seven shillings a day, all found: the cheaper lodging houses were charging one and sixpence.

The Conference began with special sermons on the Sunday and an opening meeting in the hideous modern Corn Exchange during the afternoon. On the Monday hundreds converged to an early prayer meeting, followed after breakfast by "conversational meetings" and general addresses. The atmosphere could be gauged from the "great earnestness of purpose depicted in their countenances" as men and women walked past the creeper-covered walls of ancient colleges to the Town Hall. Still worried lest "new and peculiar doctrines" were to be argued, Harford-Battersby soon noticed a difference from other religious conferences: "a definiteness of purpose . . . and a directness of aim in the speakers which was very remarkable. That purpose was . . . 'the promotion of Scriptural holiness.' The aim of the speakers, therefore, was to bring about this result by an ordered scheme of teaching out of the holy Scriptures." Each speaker seemed to build upon the last. Robert Pearsall Smith was chairman. In the afternoon Hannah gave Bible Readings, and, wrote one of the audience, "anything more impressive or delightful, now sparkling to humor, now touching to tears, we never remember hearing." Theodore Monod spoke, and old Dr. William Boardman, his accent broader, more western than that of the Pearsall Smiths.

As far as Harford-Battersby could gather, they were saying that you could have intimate companionship with Christ all day long, that God's will and your happiness were one, that the Holy Spirit and not yourself overcame your temptations; but you had to make a deliberate act of full surrender and enter a "rest of faith"—there would be a crisis leading to a process. A lady of his acquaintance met him in the street. She asked:

"Can you explain to me the teaching they are giving? Can you accept it?"

"No. I cannot," Harford-Battersby replied. "And I do not believe it is sound, or in accordance with Scripture."

On the Tuesday evening one of the two addresses came from Evan Hopkins. In the past year he had been speaking on holiness wherever opportunity offered, and on the platform of the Town Hall, in all the vigor of thirty-six, Evan Hopkins displayed a commanding sense of authority backed by personal experience. Harford-Battersby had never seen him before but felt drawn immediately by his balance, clarity of thought, grasp of Scripture.

He took the story of the nobleman whose son was sick at Capernaum and went up to Cana to beg Jesus, "Sir, come down ere my child die. Jesus saith unto him, Go thy way; thy son liveth. And the man believed . . . and went his way."

Hopkins stressed that "the nobleman who came to Christ on behalf of his son had real faith. But it was a seeking faith, carrying a burden. He came some fifteen miles to find the Lord Jesus, being fully convinced of His power to heal. Seeking faith may be intensely earnest, importunate and persevering, but may exist with great distress, anxiety and worry." And this, Hopkins pointed out, was the kind of faith common to a very large number of Christians: he had placed his finger on a fundamental weakness of Victorian religion.

"But the nobleman arrived at a point which may be called a crisis. It was the point at which a transition took place. He passed from a *seeking* faith to a *resting* faith. As soon as that step was taken his burden rolled away, his anxiety was gone. Relief came, and a calm peace filled his soul. How did this come to pass?" Christ had withheld any sign or wonder. The nobleman had no evidence, nothing except Jesus' assurance, "Thy son liveth." "This was the crisis," said Hopkins. "What did the man do when he heard this statement? Did he wait to feel sure of it, or did he take the statement as equivalent to the fact itself? 'And the man *believed* the word which Jesus had spoken, and *went his way*.' That single step changed the attitude of his faith. It was no longer seeking, with a burden. But resting, without a burden."

Harford-Battersby stirred very slightly in his seat. "I said to myself, Has not my faith been a seeking faith when it ought to have been a resting faith? And if so, why not exchange it for the latter? And I thought of the sufficiency of Jesus and said I *will rest* in Him—and I did rest in Him."

At the close of the meeting he said nothing to anyone,

friend or stranger, "afraid lest it should be a passing emotion. But I found that a presence of Jesus was graciously manifested in a way that I knew not before, and that I did *abide in Him*." Next morning, before the chambermaid knocked on his door with the early tea, Harford-Battersby woke "with a sweet sense of His blessed presence and indwelling."

At once his level-headedness reasserted itself. "I do not want to rest on these emotions but just to believe and cling to Christ as my All." And, shy and reserved though he was, he determined as a duty to God and those who had "taught this truth so persistently" to align himself with them openly before the end of the Conference.

On the Wednesday morning, at a discussion meeting, a well-known clerical dignitary who had spoken against the teaching beckoned Hopkins to leave the hall and argue privately, and they walked back to the Clarendon. They were standing talking at the door of the hotel when a man came by whom Hopkins did not know. The dignitary hailed him, and he joined the conversation. Hopkins was "struck with the clearness and force with which he supported the view brought out at the Conference. There was a remarkable expression of holy gladness in his face which convinced me that he was speaking from an actual realization of the deliverance of which he spoke." Hopkins asked the stranger his name, and "How long have you known this blessing? When did you enter into it?"

"Oh," replied Harford-Battersby, "only last night when you were speaking upon seeking and resting faith."

All over Oxford, in hotels and boarding houses, and as they walked by the river, the visitors felt themselves in a land of morning calm. Christian unity and spiritual power seemed in the very air. "I am like one that dreams," said Hopkins to a friend. "A new spirit and atmosphere for Christian life," thought a young Cambridgeshire clergyman, "a visitation of Christ in close, interested, loving helpful contact with the whole life of His disciple. The distinction between the religious and the common in Christian living vanished." A Congregational minister told Canon Christopher of St. Aldate's, Oxford: "I came here full of prejudices against the clergy of the Established Church, but now these are gone forever." At one of the evangelistic open air services in the evenings an Oxfordshire yokel was heard to ask another, "What be a doing, Jarje?"

"Why, they do say that all the Christians in the world are to be one sect."

During the night of Thursday to Friday, September 3–4, Harford-Battersby could not get to sleep. After a while he ceased to try. "My mind was dwelling on the truths I had heard, and on the Lord Jesus," he told a friend eight years later. "As the hours passed the presence of the Lord grew more and more real till at length I had, in the vision of faith, a sight of the glory of the Lord! I cannot describe it. I wouldn't if I could! I shall never forget what I saw then, to my dying day." "A revelation of Christ to my soul so extraordinary, glorious and precious. . . . How it humbled me, and yet what peace it brought." In his diary he wrote: "I had such a solemn time of fresh surrender to God."

That evening a "ministerial experience meeting" had been arranged. The laity filled the body of the Corn Exchange, and parsons of all denominations overflowed the platform in a solid phalanx of black tipped with white stocks or collars. Any minister might announce a text and follow it by one or two sentences of personal evidence. Time fled. The next address was canceled. Man after man rose, said his few words and sat down. Several prominent acquaintances told the audience that the past days had been epochal.

Harford-Battersby rose, diffident, determined. "'See that ye refuse not Him that speaketh.' I feel most thankful to have shared in this Pentecostal season," he began, and in six sentences affirmed that he had now "seen the simplicity of this way of faith, and accepted it for myself. . . . It is a difficult thing to speak of my own experience, and very distasteful, yet perhaps for this reason it may be right to do so and to acknowledge the blessing I have received."

# Four

## "The Painful Collapse"

At Oxford Harford-Battersby met a Cumbrian neighbor. They traveled home together and became fast friends. Robert Wilson, then forty-eight, was "a man of massive frame and of great strength, bearded and burly," so Harford-Battersby's eldest son John recalls, with twinkling blue eyes and a fresh complexion, what little could be seen for the whiskers. His movements were slow, his humor deep under a solemn exterior, he was sparing in speech and, if pressed to a course he thought wrong, took refuge in Quaker silence. He owned coal mines in Cumberland and sat on railway boards, and had built himself a pleasant country house, Broughton Grange, at Great Broughton on the far side of Cockermouth, the next town northwest of Keswick on the road to Carlisle, where from the terrace in fine weather he had a panorama of Lakeland from Skiddaw to Scafell. Like many in that village a Quaker, every Sunday after Friends' Meeting in the morning he would superintend the Baptist afternoon Sunday school and go to evening service at the parish church.

The Oxford Conference deepened his sense of catholicity, threw him more on Scripture, and brought him an experience similar to that of Harford-Battersby, who in the days following Oxford warmed to the knowledge that strong, silent Robert Wilson stood quietly in support twelve or fifteen miles away.

As soon as the Vicar returned from Oxford to Keswick his principal parish worker noticed that his face was "lit up with joy and he had evidently got something he had not before, and he called his people together and told them of the wonderful blessing that he had received." He set himself also to write a paper defending and analyzing the Oxford Conference before his brother clergy, meeting at Kendal shortly, and in doing so knew he would risk not only diocesan disapproval but personal friendship. Opposition to the new movement had been gathering like a thundercloud, and none rumbled against it louder than his intimate friend, Dean Close of Carlisle, a staunch evangelical who flashed like forked lightning at any cause he believed unscriptural.

Nervous tension at the prospect reacted upon frail physique. Harford-Battersby retired to bed. Robert Wilson read the paper for him and it was well received. The incident was symbolic. Harford-Battersby in his eight remaining years neither fully overcame his nerves nor lost his reserve and self-mistrust: "I have not maintained the Christ-life as I should have done," he told himself two months after Oxford. He still littered his diary with confessions of an introspective Christian never satisfied with his growth in sanctity, but balanced now by a growing awareness that "whenever I have trusted Him I have never been disappointed in Christ."

Parishioners and friends were convinced by his altered character that "his experience was a continual basking in the Saviour's presence."

Early in March 1875 Wilson received at Broughton Grange a letter from Harford-Battersby, who had gone to the South of France for his health: "I am inviting Mr. R. P. S. to Keswick for the middle of the month of June. I do not know in the least what his engagements are or whether he will be able to come, but I have projected a series of meetings in Cumberland and think that the time named would be best. . . . It may be that you have already, in concert with Kendal friends, been arranging for something in Westmorland; if so, we might combine and try to get together a numerous assemblage to look for and wait for a blessing at God's hands. I believe that many are prepared to profit by such an opportunity if it were given. Pray write a line to say what you think. It appears to me that Keswick would be a very suitable place, but if there is a better I should be willing to yield."

Wilson replied encouragingly, busy Pearsall Smith uncertainly. Harford-Battersby fell to discussing where a conference could gather. Keswick's largest hall held only three or four hundred. They might hire a large tent, "but we must remember that the object of these meetings would be to promote the full sanctification of believers, and that the numbers might not be so large, except indeed that it is likely that many would attend from a distance. I hope we should have a good attendance from Kendal."

Harford-Battersby returned from France. Wilson wholeheartedly urged that they should proceed. No public announcement, however, had been made before they both went south at the end of May for the great Brighton Convention which was to prove the apogee of Pearsall Smith—and the beginning of his end.

Brighton Corporation placed at the disposal of the Convenors, free of charge, the Dome, the Pavilion, the Corn Exchange and the Town Hall, where packed simultaneous meetings, morning, afternoon and evening, gripped the attention of a total of at least five thousand visitors.

The Moody and Sankey London campaign had six weeks to run. Among the crowds flocking to the South Coast resort, hundreds had been stirred by Moody or had learned their own spiritual inadequacy while serving as "personal workers" in his campaigns. Others came from overseas, including thirty pastors each from Switzerland and France, seventy from Germany, where Pearsall Smith had lately toured with an extraordinary measure of success, the more impressive in that the American worked through an interpreter; the excessive strain undoubtedly contributed to the coming disaster.

The Brighton Convention was the Oxford Conference on a larger scale. The united Communion services, at which foreign pastors were invited to officiate in order to avoid denominational scruples among the British, the early morning prayer hours, the monster meetings chaired by Pearsall Smith in the Dome, and Hannah's Bible Readings combined to impart an overwhelming sense of the power of Christ to save, keep and unite. With a wide range of formal addresses and several open meetings at which any might contribute, extravagant claims occasionally were put forward, peculiar analogies used, and Smith himself let slip some unguarded statements. Aberrations seemed trivial. As Harford-Battersby wrote from Brighton, "Let the teaching, as a whole, be weighed . . . and I do not fear the result. God has been wonderfully present at these meetings, as I believe, guiding the speakers and bringing many souls into liberty and light." His son John, just turning eighteen, had intended to join the family bank: "However, as day after day for ten days I listened to the teaching, the fire kindled within me"—and he left Brighton determined to spend his life as a clergyman, making known this "personal relationship with the Saviour . . . so wonderful and satisfying."

Reports from Brighton merely exacerbated opposition to "Pearsall Smithism . . . a new peril imported from America, which," thundered the *Record*, "would substitute emotional sentimentalism and visionary mysticism for solid piety and Scriptural experimentalism founded on the Word of God." Lined up with the *Record* were weighty names, especially from the Church of England: Lord Shaftesbury, old dour Dean Macneile of Ripon, who was doyen of the evangelicals, and above all John Charles Ryle, soon to be first Bishop of Liverpool, a man whose warm humanity and intense loyalty to the Bible had lain evident in the stream of lively, terse tracts and essays, speeches and sermons which had made him the unchallenged younger leader. Ryle sprang to attack, saying that the difference between Moody's teaching and that of Brighton "is the difference between sunshine and a fog."

Harford-Battersby, from his lodgings at Brighton, answered Ryle in print, "not as a controversionalist, but as a peacemaker," a distasteful duty to a man of nervous temperament who set high store by the opinions of men he respected.

Day after day the worth of the Convention showed more evident. Harford-Battersby and Robert Wilson threw away last hesitations. They went around happily together enlisting speakers, and the public heard for the first time from the Brighton platform that "Christians of every section of the Church of God" were invited to Keswick for three days of "union meetings for the promotion of practical holiness" beginning at the end of the month, on Tuesday, June 29, to be presided over by Pearsall Smith, his wife to give the Bible Readings. The Smiths were afterwards to visit Nottingham and Leeds, for Keswick would be one conference among several. The movement was sweeping ahead.

———

Pearsall Smith's last words in the Dome on June 8, 1875 were dramatic: "The Brighton Convention has now ended, and the blessings from the Convention have begun."

A fortnight later the annual Mildmay Conference of Christian Workers, North London, met in an atmosphere charged with praise, for Moody and Sankey were still drawing thousands in different parts of London and the memory of Brighton lay fresh. At an early stage the Conference was startled by an official request for prayer "for God to avert an impending calamity to His Church." Everybody began asking, "Has Moody fallen, or Spurgeon, or Smith?" Rumor said Pearsall Smith had been summoned to an urgent private meeting with eight of his supporters, including Stevenson Blackwood, a leading civil servant and chairman of the Mildmay Conference, Lord Radstock and Evan Hopkins. James Mountain, the musician, Smith's host in North London, told friends that for several days Smith had been behaving oddly, had no appetite, frequently felt sick, suffered lapses of memory, and seemingly was on the verge of a brain storm and wrestling with some horrible fear.

Hannah had been on holiday in Switzerland. She landed at Dover ready to proceed to Keswick, only to be handed a telegram that Smith had gone abroad and was ill in Paris. She took the first boat back "and found him *thoroughly* broken down. It was very evident that he could not do any work for a long time, and I succeeded in persuading him to return as soon as possible to America." He had already sent, on June 24 or 25, his telegram to Harford-Battersby. The Smiths went to a quiet spot in North Wales and from there Hannah wrote to Mrs. Cowper-Temple, who was preparing for the second Broadlands Conference: "This is my dear husband's third attack, since our marriage, of nervous prostration, and he is very weak and suffering." They sailed for Philadelphia on July 14.

It was announced that Smith was ill; nothing more. Rumors persisted that something very ugly had been suppressed: it was whispered Pearsall Smith had committed adultery. Towards the end of the year these "painful rumors" grew so loud that the eight men who had summoned Smith issued a guarded statement admitting that "the individual referred to" had inculcated heretical and dangerous doctrines in personal conversation and that "there had been conduct which, although we were convinced that it was free from evil intentions," was such that they had demanded an end to his public activity. The mental breakdown followed. Opponents of the movement quickly pointed out that the original announcement of Pearsall Smith's withdrawal on grounds of illness had been a lie, or at least not the whole truth: "Was this an exhibition of the higher life?"

The lack of frankness, followed by a refusal to publish facts, was to saddle Keswick for years with the half-spoken belief that it sprang from a tainted source. Victorians drew very thin the line between discretion and dishonesty (though they would not have called it that) and the matter was complicated by their embarrassment in any matter relating to sex. The "Council of Eight" never revealed what Smith had done and would say no more of his "heresy" than that it concerned the Bride of Christ.

The facts have lain hidden for nearly ninety years, inviting sensational speculation, until the discovery in the Broadlands archives of Smith's own detailed confession, in a letter to Cowper-Temple, which permits the truth to be brought into the open.

And the truth is pathetic rather than shocking: the whispering of a foolish if ancient heresy or delusion to a young woman in emotional and spiritual distress, with his arm around her in his hotel room at Brighton. "I blame myself greatly," Smith admitted to Temple, but swore his intentions were "as free from the wish for adultery as were it my own child. . . . Nothing beyond this was laid to my charge. . . . I do not think my intentions would have been more pure to my own daughter."

He ought to have foreseen the effect on the young woman. She seems to have been an exhibitionist, and soon spread a colorful version of her relationship with Smith. The tale trickled back to him and, overwrought as he was from exertions on the Continent and at Brighton, alarm edged him towards derangement. He was summoned to meet the eight sponsors and asked to explain. He told them all, admitting that he had been deluded, expecting sympathy and forgiveness, and encouragement to continue his ministry.

The "Council of Eight" treated Smith as a surgeon would a cancer. They sought to be loving towards him but were ruthless towards his ministry: he must disappear.

They were sensitive to the constant criticisms that the convention movement would lead inevitably to the excesses of American "Perfectionists" who kept spiritual wives, and they could not afford to risk it to save one man from his delusion. Moreover Smith himself admitted that "I was under peculiar responsibility for perfect and transparent uprightness of walk." They may have been especially sharp because that very week England rocked with the scandal of Colonel Valentine Baker of the Hussars whose attentions to a pretty girl in a railway train near Aldershot had caused her to climb screaming onto the foot plate of the moving carriage. And they were right to be ruthless because, whatever Smith said, he still harbored his delusion as late as 1878.

The "Council of Eight" did Smith disservice by refusing to disclose the facts: he was generally believed to have done worse, and few friends other than the Temples stood by him. "These cruel slanders!" Hannah exclaimed; "It has been a cruel, cruel thing." He returned to business in Philadelphia and except for one short public appearance in Pennsylvania withdrew from Christian service. For some years he kept his personal faith but it withered. The Smiths retired to live in

England in the later eighties and Hannah took part, her old, delightful self, at the last Broadlands Conferences, and her book, *The Christian's Secret of a Happy Life,* first issued in 1875 and enlarged in 1889, sold in hundreds of thousands and brought strength and comfort wherever read. The Smiths' personal fame, however, had faded as fast as it rose, and they were best known in their last years for their brilliant children, leaders among the agnostic intellectuals, especially Logan Pearsall Smith the writer and Alys, first wife of Bertrand Russell. To Lady Mount Temple in 1890 Smith wrote: "My call in life seems to have been to sound the whole possible gamut of joy and pain."

Pearsall Smith had been mightily used "in the hands of God for reviving the spiritual life in the hearts of hundreds, and even thousands of devoted servants of Christ." His presentation of truth, however, contained dangerous elements. That he was removed before the first Keswick Convention was afterwards recognized as "the overruling providence of God."

# Five

## Courage by the Lakeside

When Canon Harford-Battersby received the shattering telegram, a mere two or three days remained before visitors would stream into Keswick.

He heard that conventions were being abandoned or postponed, that the enthusiasm of several supporters had evaporated. He was tempted. "A great misfortune," he murmured, and itched to write a cancelation. Robert Wilson arrived by the afternoon train from Cockermouth. His enormous frame filled the parsonage study with reassurance. He put an arm around the Canon's shoulder. "This disappointment," he said, "is a grand opportunity to exercise trust in God." In brief simple phrases they prayed. "And from that moment we began to *reckon* upon this trial as the commencement of blessing."

Saturday saw the first arrivals, some to hotels, others sorted into boarding houses or parishioners' homes by the organizing touch of John Postlethwaite, a Keswick resident who would act as Registrar for the next thirty years. On Sunday Harford-Battersby told a packed congregation: "The responsibility incurred by me in summoning the meeting is a very solemn one, which I accept in faith. And a great responsibility rests on you, too, in connection with them. Are you satisfied with yourself? With the condition of the Church of God? If not, will you join with me in seeking to make this Convention a season of new life and power to ourselves and to the Church."

The Convention opened with a prayer meeting on Monday evening, June 28, 1875, and continued throughout Tuesday, Wednesday and Thursday, culminating in a meeting for praise early Friday. On each full day an hour and a half of prayer preceded breakfast. Half the morning passed in "Conversational Side Meetings" in the parish schoolrooms, one being elsewhere for ladies only; the later morning all were together in "the Tent." There was a choice of a song service under James Mountain or further prayer in the afternoon, and three more general meetings, one marked "Ministerial Testimonies," before the end of the day at nine. Of this formidable program, "It is particularly requested that none should attend so many of the Meetings as to interfere with full seasons of Private Prayer and Reading of Scripture. Also that all retire to rest early."

The weather was changeable. Showers and sunshine enhanced the beauty of the setting and shadows chased across lake and hills. When Skiddaw lay wrapped in cloud, banked just above the town, and then emerged in glistening freshness, visitors imbibed the air of apartness and peace that had drawn Christians in America to the woods and the little Anglo-American group to the Alps in '73. The damp at Keswick troubled no one because Wilson had installed floor boarding for the tent. He was indefatigable, waiting on physical wants in his genial way, and he had taken a house which he filled with his guests, while others were at the parsonage.

Evan Hopkins attended the next forty-one Keswick Conventions but not the first: he had wired his apologies, no doubt being busy dealing with Smith and taking over editorship of the monthly paper which Smith had founded the previous year with the cumbrous title of *The Christian's Pathway to Power*. The Convention of 1875 was impregnated by two other personalities, together with that of the balanced, reverent calm of Harford-Battersby as Chairman.

One was Henry Francis Bowker, an elderly retired public schoolmaster.

He had been Second Master at Christ's Hospital in London, an able teacher of classics, and retained a characteristic dryness of speech and ways. He had been converted at the age of twenty-nine through the influence of his marriage and in 1846 became one of the leaders of the recently founded Young Men's Christian Association; he gave Bible Readings for years at the West End branch. He enjoyed wide connections in Church and State but in character had been severe and acid. After retirement, he heard Pearsall Smith at one of the earliest holiness meetings and at once became a leader in the movement; he is credited with coining the phrase "for the deepening of spiritual life." The change in him was vividly appreciated by two of his later Keswick friends who, dining with him, happened to notice a portrait taken some years previously; they agreed that they "had never seen a more remarkable change of expression and of Christian growth than in the comparison between the face of the portrait and that which we saw in our still living friend."

He had a vigorous intelligence which shriveled such excesses as festered in Pearsall Smith. An Australian termed Bowker a "gentleman of great influence and tact" and at the first Keswick his precise grasp of truth was invaluable at the "Conversational Side Meetings," which, he said, were "very animated, many questions of great interest and importance being put. . . . An important feature, tending to correct false impressions and remove difficulties."

The other was Hanmer William Webb-Peploe, little more than half Bowker's age, being thirty-seven. Webb-Peploe stood over six feet tall, broad and lithe.

At the time of the first Convention he held a small family living* in Herefordshire, but shortly took St. Paul's, Onslow Square, in South Kensington, an upper class area of London. He stayed forty-three years. He was a younger son of a clergyman of humble faith who had inherited Garnstone Castle in Herefordshire where he lived and worked as a "Squarson," and his mother wrote religious novels popular in their day. At Cambridge Hanmer was a youth of enormous zest, jumping and swimming for the university and being one of the very few, with his younger contemporary, the father of Field-Marshal Montgomery, to have made the famous leap up the wide steps from Trinity Great Court to the doorway of Hall.

He suffered a serious smash in the gymnasium, and the prevailing ignorance of spinal injuries kept him on his back

---

* Living: a benefice provided to an English clergyman, including the revenue attached to it.

for most of his last year at Cambridge. After some months he asked if he could compete in the University sports. His doctor thought he jested and ironically said "Yes, of course," and was excessively annoyed on hearing that Peploe had left his bed, won his events and retired to lie supine again. During this prolonged inactivity he trained his memory so well that he now quoted stretches of the Bible verbatim in the pulpit and generally gave numerical reference of chapter and verse too, thereby lengthening sermons already long.

He recovered completely from the spinal injury, but a cat scratched one of his eyes. He therefore had a glass eye (and no use for cats) which added to the effect of the preaching, for his gaze held you wherever you sat, like that of a well-painted portrait.

Webb-Peploe had not intended holy orders. Shortly after coming down from Cambridge he stayed in Derbyshire with a friend called Wright who was afterwards Secretary of the Church Missionary Society. A talk together under the stars, and an incident outside the local racecourse when a stranger thrust a tract into his hands, altered the direction of his life, and having (by family legend) raced the Bishop of Hereford, Dr. Hampden, across the episcopal park for a bottle of port, Webb-Peploe was duly ordained as curate to his father. After marrying in 1863 the daughter of a Lord Justice of Appeal he was given a family living, King's Pyon, and became known as the parson who vaulted five-barred gates.

By 1874 he had six children and a small stipend. Fourteen years "a faithful preacher of the doctrine of justification," his existence was a "constant watching, waiting and struggling to do right. . . . I had no joy for every moment, no rest in the midst of trouble, no calm amid the burdens of this life; I was strained and overstrained until I felt I was breaking down."

That year he took his family for a seaside holiday at Saltburn on the Yorkshire coast. Stevenson Blackwood was also on vacation and told him of the Oxford Conference opening that very day: "He said, 'People are coming together there to seek for a blessing, to pray for the life of rest.' He looked me in the face and said, 'Have you rest?'" When Webb-Peploe understood his meaning he replied, "That is what I long for most." A friend of Blackwood's sent daily reports from Oxford and they went into the woods and read them together.

Webb-Peploe's six-month-old son Edward Alec died at Saltburn and he carried the little coffin back alone across England in the train to bury him. His holiday spoiled, his heart sore, an unexpected Sunday ahead in his own church, he tried to prepare a sermon, choosing from the set lesson a text: "My grace is sufficient for thee." He could not concentrate. He resented "all God called upon me to bear. I flung down my pen, threw myself on my knees and said to God, 'It is *not* sufficient, it is not sufficient! Lord, *let* Thy grace be sufficient. O Lord, do!'"

He opened his eyes and saw on the wall a framed text which his mother had given him the day before he left for holiday and the servant had hung during his absence. In scrolls and squiggles and colored inks it proclaimed: "My grace is sufficient for thee." The word "is" showed up bright green. A voice seemed to say, "You fool, how *dare* you ask God to make what *is*! Get up and take, and you will find it true. When God says '*is*' it is for you to believe Him." Webb-Peploe got up. "That '*is*' changed my life. From that moment I could say, 'O God, whatever Thou dost say in Thy Word I believe, and, please God, I will step out upon it.'"

"The local farmers began to say, 'Mr. Peploe does not seem as fidgety as he used to be.'" When cows invaded the vicarage lawn or callers interrupted sermon time he no longer flared in irritation.

Webb-Peploe spoke at Brighton, and after moving to London appeared frequently on convention platforms and regularly at Keswick. The spiritual experience of 1874 and his growth thereafter did not fashion him an insipid saint but full-blooded. He had a passion for exercise, walked several miles daily through London streets, skated, played tennis until he was nearly eighty. He had an independent mind and a somewhat autocratic manner and brooked no nonsense from curates or opponents. He might have been a bishop if, as *The Times* said, "he had been gifted with more finesse and if his qualities as a statesman had been more in proportion to his obvious earnestness as an advocate." "Peploe lacks balanced judgment—he's too hasty," one of his Keswick colleagues told Robert Wilson in the nineties. He was also inclined to be prickly when principles were involved, especially if he scented detraction of the Anglican Church. "I suppose," Hopkins wrote to Wilson at a time when Nonconformists were gaining a fairer share on the Keswick platform, "Peploe will be happier if you send him the list of speakers. It is as well to *oil* the machinery as much as possible to avoid friction."

Peploe's authoritarian tendencies were mitigated by a genuine charm which captivated all ages—the young men's camps at later Keswicks preferred his visits to those of any other speaker—and by the largeness of heart which enabled him to walk off arm-in-arm with the Anglo-Catholic leader Lord Halifax after uninhibited public debate. His humor was lively, and though he never introduced funny stories, as would Moody, his sermons had a cheerfulness to balance the strong sense of the numinous; his private life, from which he excluded all that he conceived worldly, had a positive gaiety. Under all lay humility. As his grandson said, "In his own eyes he was only a sinner saved by grace, always needing the mercy of a long-suffering Lord, ever and utterly dependent on the grace of God, and useless unless abiding in Christ."

At Webb-Peploe's funeral in 1923 a flower model of an open Bible lay in his coffin, with a card in his wife's writing: "He learned it. He loved it. He lived it." The Bible was the cornerstone and content of his preaching.

He was not an academic but he had integrity of intellect, a fund of knowledge, scorn of shallow thought, and that gift of the true scholar, the power to impart deep truth in simplicity. "His use of the English language was perfect," a woman attender at Keswick remembers. "He spoke without notes and with very great penetration, and in the most moving way which went right to the heart of those who heard him. Once having listened to him you could very seldom forget what he said." He had a mellifluous voice which carried to the end of the tent without sounding raucous. He spoke as fast as Moody, and took an impish delight in defeating a shorthand reporter: "Out comes his pencil and he takes down the text but soon he stares up at me with open mouth, and then down goes his pencil, and he gives up!" Webb-Peploe's height and unaffected dignity added authority to his speech.

The audience at the first Keswick Convention soon

learned the power of this strong personality, not yet forty: "His wonderful command of Scripture," John Harford-Battersby recalls, "his strong voice, his torrential rapidity of utterance swept us along in the pursuit of truth from Genesis to Revelation, and then drove us to our knees before God in penitence, trust and adoring love."

———————

"Nothing can be imagined more simple or more 'unconventional' than the arrangements of that first holy meeting at Keswick," Webb-Peploe wrote thirty years later. "All that the speakers knew of preparation times was that after long and earnest prayer in Canon Battersby's house at night, he would apportion the next day's work and say to each one, 'Will you take this?' and 'Will you take that?' The emergency, the snatching away of human aid which organizers and visitors alike had relied upon, induced a strong sense of dependence on God."

A high level of speaking and of attention became immediately evident at the first main meeting, when Webb-Peploe sounded three distinctive notes of the Convention: the authority of Scripture, the centrality of the Cross, and the call to be practical.

Expounding from 1 Thessalonians 2: "That ye would walk worthy of God who hath called you," he demanded first whether they were "ready to bow before the Word of God. I ask you to let God speak to your souls now, directly from His Word with every prejudice and preconceived opinion laid aside." He unfolded Scripture in an eminently expository address with copious use of parallel passages to elucidate and explain. "It is written: Be ye holy, for I am holy," he quoted from First Peter, adding, "We are absolutely called to be holy after the manner and standard of God Himself. . . . Almost all Christians have been hitherto living infinitely below their privileges and calling." Then he spoke of "the purpose of the Son in dying to redeem you," and made plain, as Pearsall Smith had not, that the Cross must hold the center of teaching on holiness; and he put a question: had Christ died "simply to take away your guilt, and then leave you to walk with a sort of shuffling gait through the world, which should make the godless ones mock at your salvation?"

In the shadow of the Cross he turned to practical details of a Christian's walk. Other conventions had announced as their intention the "promotion of Scriptural holiness"; Harford-Battersby recognized that most who attended Keswick would assume Scriptural teaching, but that this could degenerate into theory divorced from realities, and he summoned his Convention, therefore, for "the promotion of *practical* holiness." Webb-Peploe's masterly survey focused his hearers on the daily purposes and power of God the Father, Son and Holy Spirit. "Consider these things on your knees," he said, "and I fear many of you will soon come to the Cross and say, 'O God, I have utterly failed to apprehend the riches of the glory of Thine inheritance in the saints,' and you will, moreover, have found out the cause of your failure."

Much of what Webb-Peploe taught, and others that followed—especially Murray Shipley, an American, and George Thornton, a Midlands clergyman—opened new vistas of Christian possibilities, new levels of personal standards, to the awareness of the stuffy, inhibited, overloaded pedestrian believers who crowded the Tent. Most of them were middle-aged or elderly—no one imagined the cohorts of the young who would later converge on Keswick. Most, or their husbands, were in ministry, lay or ordained. The first Keswick drew from all three united kingdoms, but no prominent men or women as had graced the streets at Oxford and Brighton. Controversy remained almost excluded.

Puzzlement and a spirit of inquiry battled with widening desire to get at the root of the matter. By Thursday evening, after two days of listening, asking questions, debating during strolls beside Derwent Water or on the lower slopes of Skiddaw, people were not surprised that, as Harford-Battersby wrote, "the Spirit of the Lord was mightily present, especially when Mr. Peploe was speaking on the subject of the great 'promise of the Spirit,' and of the possibility of being 'filled with the Spirit.'" When the short Convention dispersed the leaders were left in no doubt from conversations and letters that the one object had been fulfilled: "to lead the believer," as Bowker expressed it, "to yield himself wholly to Christ and to trust Him in obedience to His commands in all things. . . . These conferences or conventions attended by such large numbers show a craving of heart after some greater power of God over *self* than has been seen in the Church of God for a long season."

Harford-Battersby told a friend: "We have had a time of extraordinary blessing. More, far more, than our weak faith enabled us to grasp beforehand. . . . I can only account for it by the fact that we were so entirely thrown upon the Lord. It has been a lesson of great value to myself and my faith has been much strengthened in consequence."

# Six

## Advance Through Storm

The first Keswick was nearly the last.

Opposition reverberated noisily through months that followed. Church newspapers printed immensely long letters that must have consumed hours of ministerial time as pens scratched in country rectories and city cathedrals in the time-honored tradition of British theological debate—furiously condemning what had not been heard or experienced at firsthand. "The fact was," Webb-Peploe wrote in afteryears, "that they did not know what was really being taught by sober, earnest and spiritually-minded men; they only formed their opinions from certain mistaken reports of a claim to the entire eradication of sin."

The movement was not without a few influential voices such as Wace, the Dean of Canterbury, and the Presbyterian Andrew Bonar of Glasgow, openly contradicting his brother Horatius Bonar, whose opposition seemed inconsistent with the words of his own hymn, "Fill Thou my life . . . in every part with praise." There were Anglicans to point out that the teaching harmonized with scores of lines in the Book of Common Prayer, such as "keep us this day without sin," "walking from henceforth in His holy ways," and the collect for the Ninth Sunday after Trinity: "Grant to us, Lord, we beseech Thee, the spirit to think and do always such things as be rightful; that we, who cannot do anything that is good without Thee, may by Thee be enabled to live according to Thy will." In the middle of the controversy, in October 1875, the great Congregationalist leader R. W. Dale of Birmingham ranged himself, rather gingerly, in support: "If any man can tell me how the heavens above me are to become brighter, how my peace is to become deeper, how my strength is to be augmented, I will thank him for telling me and I will not be too critical about the way in which he tells it to me." Dale realized that the movement's adherents had not yet adequately defined their experience. He scorned, however, the illogicality of their detractors who taught converted drunkards or adulterers to "trust God perfectly for strength to overcome" gross vices but told moral men with little sins "to fight and struggle," and were not alarmed if a Christian remained bad-tempered twenty years.

Encouragement from such as Dale was a shaft of sunlight through a black sky. The more usual attitude was expressed in the outburst of an eminent evangelical clergyman who, chairman of a clerical meeting which Webb-Peploe addressed in characteristically Scriptural and reasoned terms, "rose as soon as I had finished, and said: 'Heresy! *Heresy*!! Damnable heresy! I hold that it is for the glory of God that we should fall into sin, that He may get honor to Himself by drawing us out of it!'"

When at the end of 1875 the public at last learned that

Pearsall Smith's withdrawal had not been occasioned by health alone, the *Record* hailed the "Collapse of Pearsall Smithism" with ill-concealed glee and expected to hear no more of conventions at Keswick or elsewhere. Harford-Battersby saw that to continue "will be to expose myself to still warmer and fiercer hostility. . . . If I make a mistake in this, my whole future influence in the Church and ministry will be compromised. It is no light or trifling matter." He determined to rethink his position, ready either to acknowledge error or to "stand fast as a rock, trusting in Him." Webb-Peploe wrote from Herefordshire to Hopkins at Richmond in the spring of 1876: "I do not know what you find among your more intelligent folk, but down here, even among orthodox Evangelicals, I am looked upon as 'half a black sheep.' This is the trial of our faith, I suppose, for one would expect true brothers to have an understanding heart. They ask me to preach but look half-askance and are afraid of what is taught. They cannot deny it but dare not, it would seem, accept it with humble boldness and faith. God help us all! . . . Let us go on our way rejoicing even if we are called to suffer shame for His name's sake."

Announcement of a second Keswick dallied until early May. July 31 until August 4 was the chosen period, and the weather sided with those who wished to blow the Convention into the sea: "excessive rain, with thunder and lightning and violent storms of wind, resulting on the third day in the overthrow of our beautiful tent." It collapsed in the night. Wilson heard the noise from his rented house, rose, dressed, and spent until sunrise transferring benches and chairs single-handedly to the Drill Hall in time for the 7 a.m. prayer meeting. "The result was, however," Webb-Peploe recalled, "somewhat trying for us speakers, specially for Mr. Hopkins and myself; as we had to rush from the Drill Hall to the Lecture Hall, and vice versa, all day long, repeating our addresses alternately in each."

Little was heard in the press, national or religious, of the Keswicks of 1876 and 1877. "We went to Keswick more or less with the feeling that we were losing our reputation in doing so," wrote J. J. Luce of Gloucester a quarter of a century after, "especially if it happened to be a ministerial reputation. We were speckled birds. We were associated with those who were looked down upon, and frowned upon, to a considerable extent, and our doctrines were much criticized as well as ourselves." Only strength of conviction and reality of experience could withstand this obloquy, which served to burn away shallow thinking or false claims and to forge bonds of love and trust between the leaders. Indeed Evan Hopkins commented to Wilson, a little extravagantly, in the nineties: "Our best days were those in which we had most opposition."

For any who came once or again for the few days in the Lakeland summers of the later seventies "there was," wrote Luce, "an indescribable charm in the novelty of these early Conventions, an avidity after truth, a keen and clear understanding of what we were after, an eagerness to get 'the blessing.'" There was informality, "a remarkable absence of planning and organizing" of speakers. They came with whatever Scriptural messages had been impressed upon them as they thought and prayed beforehand, and their addresses were not such finished products as they became. Assembling for a meeting, people did not know who would address them, and this was deliberate: more meetings were arranged than everybody could or should attend. "People suited themselves as to time," was a memory of 1878, "the names of the appointed speakers being concealed, to prevent the soul anticipating either pleasure or disappointment in connection with *man*."

This muting of the human element was a factor slowly bringing forward Keswick as Great Britain's leading convention. The word "convention" gained currency to denote a particular kind of public gathering. It was interchangeable at first with "conference": Perth, Mildmay and Broadlands were "conferences" throughout their history. Moody used to summon a "Christian Convention" at the close of each major city campaign to discuss important questions, "convention" being simply American for "conference" and probably used as such by Pearsall Smith when he first came to England. Many of the local conventions which sprang up at Smith's touch did not disappear with him but were reconvened year by year, and before long a convention normally implied a special gathering for "the deepening of spiritual life" or "the promotion of practical holiness."

One of the early leaders wittily suggested that "a conference has a subject but a convention has an object." "The speakers aim at inducing *definite* personal dealing with God," wrote Hay Aitken, then the foremost Anglican evangelist, "with a view to the reception of some definite, personal, and spiritual acquisition. . . . This, I think, is what differentiates Keswick from other conferences where there is much good and eloquent speaking that leads up to nothing in particular, except a general feeling that it is all very good and very 'nice.'"

In the seventies Keswick already had a particular quality that was to be of vital importance in the eighties, enabling it to survive the shipwreck of the Holiness movement and safely convoy a spiritual treasure that undoubtedly otherwise would have been sunk, to the Church's impoverishment. This was the quality of objectivity. Many local conventions emphasized human experience. Keswick speakers focused on Christ. "The Message given at Keswick," one writer pointed out, "searches heart and conscience, not by turning attention inward to questions of subjective experience, but upward to the glory of Christ's Person, the efficacy of His atonement, and the sufficiency of His grace for all needs in the 'daily round and common task' of Christian life and service."

To the Keswick of 1878 came a thick-bearded visitor from Australia. Hussey Burgh Macartney was an Irishman from Trinity College, Dublin, who had emigrated with his father, the first Dean of Melbourne, and became Vicar of Caulfield, a suburb of Melbourne.

He did more than any man to promote Australian interest in the Church Missionary Society, and afterwards in the China Inland Mission too. In 1874–75, when he read of Oxford and Brighton, he promptly organized similar conventions in Victoria. He was a man of peculiarities. A tireless walker, with an oriental sense of time and almost complete indifference to food or sleep, "he went everywhere with a child's simplicity, and you delighted to turn domestic arrangements upside down for his benefit." One of his hobbies was to cram words on a postcard to make a condensed letter—he could achieve nearly three hundred words. He loved good stories and unmalicious gossip and would have made a fine columnist. The impression of Keswick in his unconventional book *England, Home and Beauty* (1879) forms one of the earliest independent records.

"Canon Battersby and Mr. R. Wilson were on the platform to meet the train," he wrote. "I soon found myself in the most delightful quarters at St. John's parsonage, and sitting among some twenty friends whom Canon and Mrs. Battersby had gathered round their table." The Convention opened that evening, Monday, July 27, with the customary prayer meeting. The spacious marquee (still the diocesan tent) was "pitched in a green field, well-lighted, floored and seated, with a large platform for speakers, reporters and singers, and capable of holding a thousand persons." The singing was led by James Mountain from the little hymn book compiled in 1875 by himself and Pearsall Smith (whose name had been dropped), *Hymns of Consecration and Faith*. It lasted until 1890, by then being reckoned "undoubtedly too esoteric and subjective"; Mrs. Evan Hopkins compiled a new, larger edition under the same name. Appropriate new hymns continually were appearing, such as *Thou Whose Name Is Called Jesus* and *Jesus, I Am Resting, Resting*, both written since Brighton by an Irish woman, Jean Sophia Piggott, of whom little is known except that she attended Keswick in 1879 and died in 1882.

Macartney, who made a highly effective contribution to the Keswick of 1878 by his brief addresses at the early morning prayer meetings, thought the Convention arrangements "perfect—a secretary to find accommodation for visitors in hotels or lodgings; an inquiry office; cloak room and refreshment room; a bookstall at the gate," and Harford-Battersby's parishioners seemed to have excelled themselves in frequent hospitality at their own cost. Everything was under "the constant and careful attention of Mr. R. Wilson, a wealthy, warmhearted, single-minded Christian man, with great business capacity, who made everybody's wants his own."

Macartney's thumbnail sketches bring early Keswick speakers to life: Harford-Battersby, "a man to love, and respect and admire; still, calm, and always accessible in the middle of the week's heavy responsibilities; wise, prudent, and without partiality." Old Haslam, who had propelled Harford-Battersby to Oxford four years before: "his bright eyes nearly blind, but quoting text and chapter and verse as if his Bible were open before him, and dispelling with easy power the mists that Satan makes to gather round the Cross, and around the life of faith, and around the life beyond." And Boardman, the American whose book had, in a sense, begun it all, now living in England: "calm, solid, strong, earnest, kind—but not in word or presence the fiery torch you would imagine him to be from his glowing writings."

Evan Hopkins, Richmond vicar and editor of *The Christian's Pathway to Power*, "quite a young man, was there in his happiest frame, unraveling difficulties, removing misapprehension, and stating such truths as concerned Christians with singular exactness."

Hopkins, now nearly forty-one, had reached his prime and now must come forward to the center of the scene.

# Seven

## Hopkins and His Team

Evan Henry Hopkins, of Welsh extraction, had been born in South America, educated in Australia, and afterwards at the School of Mines in London. He never lost the wanderlust—though its solace had to be Continental holidays and two visits to Palestine and Egypt, once he had abandoned his father's profession of civil engineer to take holy orders in 1865.

He had been a slum curate under a High Church parson in London's dockland, and then moved to the congenially evangelical staff of Portman Chapel in the West End, where he had to prepare his occasional sermons knowing that the great Lord Shaftesbury would lend a critical ear. Hopkins was appointed to Holy Trinity, Richmond, in 1871 and remained until 1893, when he took the living of St. Luke's, Redcliffe Square, in Kensington.

The formative experience at the Curzon Chapel on May Day, 1873, brought him the chief interest and concern of his ministry. At the twelve conferences held annually at

Broadlands until Lord Mount Temple's death, as well as at Keswick, at lesser conventions, and at the afternoon holiness meetings in public rooms in London, Evan Hopkins was a foremost speaker and assiduous in committee. He did not neglect his parish. His abounding energy made Holy Trinity Church a citadel of aggressive evangelism and he was the unacknowledged virtual founder of the Church Army, which began at Richmond as the "Church Gospel Army" after Hopkins and his wife had become enthused with Salvation Army mission methods. The young Wilson Carlile had been one of his zealous parishioners before his own ordination, and adapted and enlarged the scheme.

Hopkins was conspicuous for black hair and whiskers, and square-cut features, but these became ponderous as he grew older. He had average height: "You wouldn't look at him a second time, as you would Webb-Peploe" is a younger man's memory. He was a little reserved. But, wrote W. Y. Fullerton, "When I came to know the man I found he was much greater than either his writings or his speech." His organist for over thirty years called his "a truly lovable nature" and could remember "never a harsh word."

Undoubtedly Hopkins had a placid temperament. His serenity, however, under opposition, disappointment, fatigue, could not be ascribed merely to nature. He taught Christians to expect the Holy Spirit to give them serenity, and his own life made the teaching credible. To some who saw him only on the platform in old age "he did not seem a particularly happy man," but the impression was belied by the evidence of his intimates. "He always saw the funny side of things," wrote the daughter of a Keswick speaker. "I was so afraid that to be a wholly surrendered Christian might mean to wear a bow-bonnet and never smile again! I never thought so after I knew Mr. Hopkins." He was a good raconteur, could turn effortlessly from light-hearted to grave, and if any doubted his sense of humor they need only look at his comic pen-and-ink rabbits.

Hopkins had varied gifts. His watercolors were well up to the standard of the Victorian amateur, he could amuse himself by writing the Lord's Prayer in a circle the size of a sixpence; it would be interesting to know if Macartney and Hopkins had a competition. He was a little of a bird watcher and, curiously, had a strong dislike of shrubs. His scientific abilities were considerable. He experimented with the de-magnetizing of ships, and in 1902 patented a process of zinc distillation which unfortunately proved without commercial possibilities. He read widely in science. He spoke several languages and, when past sixty, learned Hebrew, courageously but unsuccessfully attempting a Durham B.D.

Evan Hopkins' best gift to Keswick was the application of a scientific mind: on the platform, in private conversations, in columns of *The Christian's Pathway to Power* (which he reorganized as the monthly *Life of Faith* in 1879, handing the publishing to his parishioner A. H. Marshall in 1883) and especially behind the scenes.

His preaching owed nothing to oratorical arts. None of the Celt in him obtruded; as somebody said, "He gave bread, not confectionery." He spoke quietly, with a slightly husky, well-sustained, even voice, dividing his matter carefully and amassing fact and argument in the manner of an advocate persuading a judge, not a forensic genius dazzling a jury. "He was saturated in the Scriptures," wrote a young Scot, "great in analysis, in distinguishing between things that differed and in separating the essential from the accidental. He seemed to have an intimate knowledge of the real difficulties that lay in the way of receiving the Convention message, and to have ready at hand the answer." Sometimes he overstrained a text, but never to adduce an unscriptural doctrine. His overwhelming May Day experience and the sudden bursting of sunshine on scores of others, such as Harford-Battersby, inclined him to speak as if the deepening of a genuinely converted Christian's spiritual life could begin only through a second crisis, but he always taught this crisis to be the beginning of a process. "Remember," he said constantly, "the Blessing is not an attainment but an attitude."

He loved illustrations. "He constantly laid stress," wrote Eugene Stock of the C.M.S., "upon the necessity for Christians to *walk on two feet*, 'faith' and 'surrender.' It was he who again and again reminded them that a dislocated ankle could never be put right by trying and trying to walk; that it must be set, with the result of instant relief. This *setting* was a momentary act, accomplished by the Holy Ghost in response to faith, but this once done, the process of gaining strength for walking would be easy."

Whoever was Chairman of Keswick, Hopkins remained the power behind the chair. And in the tragically difficult days to come his clarity and balance would do more than any other man, save one, to steer Keswick through the shoals. "He guided us along the pathway of truth," John Harford-Battersby said, "and guarded us from taking the bypaths which tempted men to turn aside to the right hand or the left."

There would come a period when it would be regrettably possible to speak of a Keswick "type." The early speakers were not of a type. None could be more diverse than Harford-Battersby the shy, cultured ex-Tractarian, Bowker the learned schoolmaster, Webb-Peploe the athlete squire, and Hopkins the scientist.

Others were emerging to join them. Some came occasionally, such as the foreigners Theodore Monod the Frenchman and Otto Stockmeyer the Swiss pastor, whose somewhat involved mystical mind and imperfect command of English kept his addresses from wide appeal but rewarded patient hearers; and the whole Convention was moved the evening when Stockmeyer "led the people in audible prayer of deep humiliation that he, personally, had given such poor testimony that day of what the Lord was able to do."

The bulk of the speaking came from a small group who, contrary to later practice, held the platform with Hopkins and Webb-Peploe year after year unless ill or absent abroad. One of them, first heard at the Keswick of 1879, was Charles Armstrong Fox.

If any mortal had a right to be moody and sad it was Charles Fox. A year older than Hopkins and Webb-Peploe, he had overstrained his health at Cambridge, where he was a Hebrew prizeman, and collapsed after a year or two's curacy in the Devonshire countryside. He retired with his young wife to a tiny cottage near Tiverton, unable for ten years to do more than a minimum for the ministry to which he was passionately devoted. By nature he was impatient, quick in retort and wounding in satire. Yet instead of gloom and sarcasm and irritability, the cottage household exuded, in the words of a neighboring clergyman, "merry thoughts. . . .

The mirth and fun were never absent from any of our talks. From his light merriment he could turn perfectly naturally, and one never felt that there was any want of harmony between the two phases."

Fox recovered sufficiently to take work in London, laughingly saying he was only a "maimed curate," in 1873. He recognized quickly the emerging Holiness movement to be teaching what he had learned already in affliction, and in aiding it his faith so increased that for a time he believed one of his most grievous handicaps to have been removed: an irregular but tongue-tying stammer. This was not quite so, but he discovered how to refute it, and when an audience listening to him in full flood saw the vigorous gesture of throwing forward both arms, close friends knew that Fox was warding off the stammer. "How few," wrote a fellow speaker, "could dream that when, in pulpit or platform, he was thrilling us with his deep and loving words, he was often fighting a physical battle merely to speak them."

After hearing Fox at Brighton in 1875 Harford-Battersby had said: "You are the very man we want. Will you come?" Illness prevented him and the Keswick of 1879 was his first, his attendance being unbroken for eighteen years. Behind this record lay constant ill-health. He never revealed publicly "how much I have to practice direct and determined trust in God for the body, and that I could never speak at all if I did not launch myself upon God for the power to do it."

It seemed unbelievable to those who saw him in public. He was virile, sparkling. A Keswick colleague affirmed he had "never known any case in which the joyous fun of a strong man was so absolutely in harmony with Christian feeling." Fox would hail an acquaintance in the street, probably make him laugh, then leave him a flash of Biblical insight that would embolden faith the rest of the day. An address would bring his hearers right to the foot of the Throne. As he walked back afterwards his companions would be unaware of his utter exhaustion, the pain surging across his body; his instinctive reaction was "glancing wit and quick shaft of fun to enable him to endure and to cover up what he felt." He would retire to another night of insomnia or fitful sleep. Each new day seemed a veritable resurrection.

The nature of his malady is not evident. It must have been basically nervous, but that he was no hypochondriac is plain from the dreadful suffering that closed his life.

Fox to a high degree had a gift of sympathy, especially for the defeated or despairing: "He was one to whom the need presented to him—sorrow, anxiety, perplexity or whatnot—became absorbing and at once important. He thought and felt fully with his neighbor. And he showed that this was no superficial sweetness by the faithful memory of it all which was sure to come out when you met him next." Bishop Handley Moule spoke of his "personal attraction, not least in private; the charm of his irresistible sympathy, the beautiful blend of high and wide culture with the most unmistakable walk with God." Fox never received full recognition from the general public, either as a preacher at Eaton Chapel in the heart of Belgravia, of which he was incumbent for twenty-six years, or as a poet. Poetry bubbled from his every vein, the slightest experience turned easily to verse. To a later generation his poems read rather like Wordsworth on an off-day, and many he published he ought to have discarded, but they were genuine in expression and feeling. He did not easily write hymns. His few died with his generation.

Fox admired the Lake Poets fervently, as did Harford-Battersby, and shared their love of nature. On holiday he would walk miles in the Scottish Highlands whenever health permitted. The scenery of the Lake District was his joy. Dundas Harford-Battersby the younger remembers being with him "beside a tarn in the Coniston valley. He rhapsodied and parabolized on every cloud and ripple and growth. I said, 'Are you justified in turning these things into parables?' His reply has entered into the warp and woof of one's mind. 'My dear boy, the parables *are there*. It is our duty to find them.'"

His first address at the Keswick of 1879 followed Pastor Stockmeyer's grave solemnity, "which made one almost shrink from what yielding wholly to Christ might involve. Then by the side of this almost ascetic gravity, there was Mr. Fox, with the joyous spirit of a child reveling in his Father's garden, showing you all its fragrant flowers and fruit, making them so accessible." Fox spoke smoothly, almost extemporarily, for writing was a physical burden. His addresses were not analytical or closely expository but were vivid with natural images and illustrations, for he was a man who thought in pictures. He emphasized human weakness and divine power, the need of unbroken humiliation if the divine wealth would be known. He had the touch to make his hearers feel themselves "naked and open to the eyes of Him with whom we have to do," and on the Thursday evening of 1879, as he spoke on the text: "Except a corn of wheat fall into the ground and die, it abideth alone; but if it die, it bringeth forth much fruit," "an awe of God fell upon the whole assembly, in a way the writer [in 1895] has never since seen equaled"; "*If it die! If it die!*" echoed Fox. "Is the reason of the solemn loneliness of your life, without fruit in other souls, just this, that you have not been content to die? *If it die! If it die!* Then let that echo on and on, until the self-life finds its place, and keeps its place, in the death and the grave of Jesus."

Thereafter he was always given the last address on the last night of each Convention. "He would spend the day in communion with God," writes John Harford-Battersby, "and would come forth with shining face to proclaim the glories of his Lord, and to summon us to seek the highest."

Fox had been in the movement from the beginning. So had the Irishman from Brighton, John Bradley Figgis of the Countess of Huntingdon's Connection, first non-Anglican to be a regular Keswick speaker, "gentle, spiritual, deep and yet so simple," who had a "high shrill voice. . . . By the aid of vivid words, passionate appeals and abundant gestures he held the complete attention of his audience." And Hubert Brooke, a vicar in Reading, Berkshire, whom Bowker heard give Bible Readings and invited to Keswick in 1881. From that year Brooke established the custom of the morning Bible Reading. Figgis said of him: "His style, clear as a frosty night and bright as its stars, as full of vivacity as of solemnity, exactly suited the light touch of topic after topic from page to page, and book to book, of the wonderful Word of God. His argument, so forcible that it holds you in its grip, and his illustrations so sunny that it attracts you by its radiance, must have made some of his hearers feel—I never knew there was so much in the Bible." Macartney said his voice had "a peculiar quality—you *must* listen to it."

A feature of the early years was the accession of Christian leaders to the team who when first they came to Keswick were either out of sympathy with its aims or had distinct reservations. Each Convention had a fair proportion of those who passed through the categories which Hopkins classified as "Puzzled," "Provoked" and "Persuaded."

One of the most notable of such was James Elder Cumming, D.D., a salty middle-aged minister of the Church of Scotland in Glasgow. Moody had thought him the "most cantankerous Christian I had ever met." A shattering bereavement had thickened his skin, he was a fearsome theologian who delighted in shriveling opponents, yet could look back on a genuine evangelical conversion and ruled himself, he thought, with the strictest rectitude. In the summer of 1882, "I unexpectedly found an idle fortnight. Wondering what I was to do with it, there met my eye an advertisement of the Keswick Convention," which reminded him of the casual remark of a woman whose name he could not remember: "I think the best and most solemn of all these conferences is the one that is held at Keswick."

He wrote to Postlethwaite, engaged a room and went alone: "As far as I knew there was not a soul in all the Convention that I was likely to be acquainted with." On the first evening he set off for the Tent. "As he walked along," his daughter Jenny records, "a lady crossed over and accosted him, 'Are you Dr. Elder Cumming of Glasgow?' 'I am.' 'Thank God to see you here,' she replied, and walked off. 'This seems a rather queer place I have come to,' he said to himself, and went on. Round the corner another unknown lady came up and spoke to the same effect. He was amused and bewildered: 'There's no doubt this is a very queer place.'"

He took a back seat in the Tent. "What are they trying to say? They are all very faulty in their theology. All except that parson with the black hair. I follow him. He is a theologian."

"I cannot," he said thirteen years later, "tell you what pain and misery I experienced during the first three days—first, something like indignation. Secondly, something very like perplexity, for my theological chart seemed to have certain things laid down, and I did not see how other things could be put in without disarranging the former." Hopkins had noticed the "Scots D.D., who might mean so much if he came right out," and, so he once told Jenny, was "quietly praying." On the third evening Cumming accosted the black-haired parson at the tent door. "You're a theologian, like myself; but I'm puzzled about some things. Can you help me?"

Back in his little bedroom in the boarding house after their conversation he faced his past, and "the Lord told me, while on my knees in my solitude, of this, and this, and this. In perfect simplicity and innocence I said, 'Lord, these are not sins.' The answer came by His Spirit, 'Whatever they are, are they worthy of a son of God?' And at once I had to say 'No!' 'Are you willing to put them away?' 'Yes, Lord.'" Cumming got pencil and paper and made a list.

At the next aftermeeting (Hopkins believed aftermeetings to be as important, rightly used, to a convention as inquiry meetings to a mission) Cumming did not rise in silent witness, as seeker, or as finder, nor did he stay to volunteer a contribution to the ministerial testimony meeting which was held on the Saturday after the close of the Convention proper. The moment he reached Glasgow, "I rushed off without delay" to make an overdue apology, fearing he would balk at the humiliation unless he plunged, and on the Monday morning he referred warmly to Keswick in a speech at a Presbyterian gathering where "Keswick was not a pleasant name to be spoken." That afternoon, "almost for the first time in my life," he was aware of "the joy of the Lord."

The following November Cumming arranged a convention at Glasgow, with Bowker as chairman and Hopkins chief speaker, supported by Figgis and Harford-Battersby. This was the first of the annual conventions to derive directly from Keswick. Elder Cumming spoke from the platform at Keswick every year thereafter until 1906. Moody returned to Glasgow in 1891. "Whatever has happened to Cumming?" he asked. "I have never seen a man so altered, so full of the love of God." "Oh, he's been to Keswick." And Moody, who until then had remained cautious about the Convention, said promptly: "Then I only wish all other Christians would go to Keswick too, and get their hearts filled with the love of God."

One who did stand at an aftermeeting during the Keswick of 1882 was already internationally known: Andrew Murray.

Andrew Murray the younger, half-Scots, half-Boer, minister of the Dutch Reformed Church in South Africa, had for years been prominent as pastor, teacher, theologian, ecclesiastical statesman, educationalist, politician. He had been leader in a notable revival at the Cape as far back as 1860, had then founded an annual Ten Days of Prayer, with characteristics similar to Keswick, and had written in 1864 the Dutch version of a book which, when published in 1882 in English as *Abide in Christ*, had immense sale; he admitted afterwards that "I had not then experienced all I wrote of."

Murray visited England in 1882 seeking a cure for a throat

affliction. He stayed at a faith-healing home lately opened in London by Boardman, with considerable effect, and being a regular reader of the *Life of Faith* gravitated to Keswick as a listener. At Boardman's he had made a fresh surrender to Christ, "not only as my healer but as the Power of an entirely new life." When he reached Keswick, "I was holding fast the promise but without the joy and love which must in due time follow." He rose at the aftermeeting on the Tuesday "to testify my desire." When the chairman asked those to rise who had proved Christ in His fullness Murray remained seated. On Wednesday his spiritual mists lifted. "I saw it all— Jesus cleansing, Jesus filling, Jesus keeping," and at the Saturday meeting he gave "my grateful testimony to the love of our blessed Lord, and what He has done for me at Keswick."

Murray was not a man of crises. His Keswick experience of 1882 seemed, in perspective, one more short step forward. But it had considerable repercussions in South Africa, England and America.

---

By the Convention of 1882, the eighth, "Keswick" was firmly established, influence increasing. Wilson had chosen its motto: *All one in Christ Jesus.* The site in Eskin Street had been bought, Wilson paying two-thirds of the £375 18s. 3d., and Harford-Battersby one-third. It was walled in April and first used in July. They rented the diocesan tent for the last time, that winter buying their own which seated, off the speakers' and choir platform, about six hundred—a somewhat curious figure, because the Convention of 1882 was reported to have drawn over twelve hundred to some of the afternoon meetings, to which day-visitors flocked by special trains from Carlisle and Barrow, and all the northwest; six hundred probably represented those who stayed for the duration. By 1886 the Tent had to be enlarged to hold nine hundred, and two years later a really large one was bought to seat 2250.*

1882 was Harford-Battersby's last Keswick.

No one foresaw, for his health was now good and he was approaching only his sixtieth birthday. He presided in the Tent, and at the open celebrations of Holy Communion in the parish church on the Sundays; on the second Sunday three hundred and sixty-seven persons of all denominations took the Sacrament.

The following spring he overworked and lay ill until July. On the opening day of the Keswick of 1883 he died, and thus, as he would have wished, was attended to his grave by the entire Convention in very lovely weather. By a pleasing providence his widow was laid beside him during the Convention of two years later.

* Convention Lodge, adjoining the Eskin Street site, was bought in 1888, and the present office, inquiry bureau, etc., was added in 1892. The Post Office was installed in 1905, and the letter box inserted in the outer wall. (The letter box cost £2-10-0 plus 2/6 carriage!)

# Eight

---

# The Edge of the Precipice

"The Dawn of a Wonderful Revival is rising upon us. . . . I know nothing in all the history of the Church like it since the end of the first 300 years of the Christian era." The Editor of the *Life of Faith* in his issue for April 1883 put into words the quickened feelings of thousands.

Moody and Sankey had been about again since the autumn of 1881, giving nearly a year to Scotland and, in the winter and spring of 1882–83, passing from city to city of England and Wales. Their mission would culminate in an eight-month campaign in different parts of London beginning in November 1883. Bowker, in his report on the Convention of July 1883, wrote: "The tide of blessing is rising all over the land. The Spirit of God is doing great things in the conversion of souls, and in leading the Church onward to a truer walk of purity and fellowship with the Lord."

Across a nation stirred by the preaching of Moody, by Sankey's heartmoving *The Ninety and Nine* and *Man of Sorrows*, by the crowds of all classes that flocked to the vast meetings, by a wave of sacred song that invaded even street corners and pubs, and the quickening as hundreds of converts joined churches in city and countryside eager to serve and learn, two streams flowed strongly. One was a desire for full consecration to God in untrammeled service; the other a longing for purity of heart: a passionate reaching to understand and experience the Biblical phrases translated: "Be ye perfect," "Be ye holy." Keswick had propounded these themes of Consecration and Purity for the past eight years, but Keswick formed merely one segment in a widespread and uncoordinated Holiness movement which was a welter of meetings, conventions, processions—many displaying excesses of religious emotion.

The heresy of Sinless Perfection rapidly gained adherents among those who could not stomach the human paradox well expressed by Monod: "We ought not to sin, and we need not sin, but as a matter of fact we do sin," and who went around teaching that "the believer's conflict with sin is all stuff!"—plain nonsense! "When the soul is filled with God," a man solemnly told H. B. Macartney, "and occupied with God rather than sin, sin is not present in the soul, because its presence is not *felt*." The danger of such people, Macartney commented, lay in their undoubted devotion and outward saintliness: "Their holy lives act like sledgehammers to drive the error home." There were humbugs aplenty, it being fatally easy to rattle off Holiness jargon; but the worst trouble came from the sincere who were unable to distinguish between feeling and fact until they slipped over the precipice or led others into spiritual disaster—either of reaction, nervous breakdown, loss of faith, or of perversion.

The Keswick leaders were considered to "have advanced

views as to Sanctification," and in the context of the times they made a daring, pioneering group. Yet Hopkins, Webb-Peploe, Fox, Bowker were holding hard on the reins as the coach of Holiness galloped towards the edge. Keswick's soberness contrasted with the Hallelujahs: "All the meetings have been particularly quiet," was the *Record*'s account one year. "There are no loud Salvationist outcries." The apartness and beauty of the Lakes were assets. When Bowker, whom Wilson with characteristic self-effacement appointed Chairman after Harford-Battersby's death, suggested they had better move the Convention elsewhere lest the next vicar oppose, the others were horrified: "God manifestly brought us to Keswick," they cried. "It would show lack of faith to leave it."

Chairman and leaders were eminently practical. "You have not perfection in man," Webb-Peploe would say, "but you have a perfect Saviour. . . . Never be afraid of drawing too near perfection, you may be sure there will always be limitations in *you*." They did not like the subjective phrase "a clean heart," which, though Scriptural, had been given dangerous overtones by the Salvation Army, then a few years old and at its most colorful and emotional. Certain other speakers at Keswick, however, drew perilously close to implying sinless perfection of the flesh, and on occasions offered entire sanctification in what a later age would call a "package deal." "There has been cause at times," a Keswick leader wrote some fifteen years later, "to take care lest one glorious side of truth should be so exclusively presented as to be deflected into error."

One who spoke dangerously from the platform in early days, although later wise and trusted, was Edward W. Moore, incumbent of Curzon Chapel, Mayfair, and subsequently of Emmanuel, Wimbledon. During the Moody and Sankey London Campaign, on a Saturday (Moody's day off) in March 1883, Moore was a fellow guest with D. L. Moody at a small private dinner in Cavendish Square, and the conversation, recorded that night by the American D. W. Whittle, reveals something of the contemporary atmosphere, pressures and problems.

Moody knew Webb-Peploe and Hopkins. He appreciated their aid. He remembered, too, as if it were yesterday, his formative moment of consecration and "baptism of the Holy Spirit" in New York in November 1872. He told the dinner party of efforts "to get me to make public profession of having the blessing of Holiness. But as I understand Hopkins, he admits the two natures, and means by the 'blessing of sanctification' an inward peace of soul resting upon Christ. I *hope* to have this. I *think* I have—"

"I am *sure* you have, Mr. Moody," interrupted Moore ("who seems a very sincere, unaffected, consecrated man"). "We all know you have."

"I know you men are way beyond me in the sweetness and peace of your daily lives," Moody went on, "and I wish I were more like you, but I *dare not* make any professions of being holy. I have peace in Christ and I trust Him, but I don't know what I might be left to do, and I never trembled more in thinking of the power of the devil and my own weakness than now. And for a man to make a profession that he is without sin, and then fall, is an awful stumbling block."

He mentioned Pearsall Smith, and referred to the duplicity of a Christian leader (unconnected with Keswick) who had leased a public house on terms legally binding him to sell spirituous liquors, in order to turn it teetotal. "'X' could do that and then go to a Holiness meeting and profess perfection!"

Moody pressed that here was the crux of the "whole doctrine of perfection: What is the standard? 'X' makes his own conscience or consciousness the standard, and does things God's law and man's law condemn as wrong, and yet claims to be without sin. Right there it seems to me is the danger of the teaching."

Moore, Whittle records, then spoke of "receiving the blessing he terms a 'clean heart' at a Salvation Army Holiness meeting four years ago. He had for some time taught Sanctification, but that night he experienced a sense of the presence of God beyond anything he had ever known." Moore said, "Since that time I have been kept in uniform peace, and the old temptations to inward pride have troubled me only occasionally, and then from the outside. I could not say I have been without sin, or that I am without sin. No, I could not say that."

Whittle asked how he knew the temptations came "from the outside."

"Well, there is a difficult point," replied Moore. "I cannot say that I positively know that they do."

"Do you believe, Mr. Moore, in the 'two natures'?"

"In a modified form I do. . . ." And they fell into an amicable inconclusive argument on the meaning of the "flesh," "the Spirit."

Neither Moody nor Moore were clear in their doctrine of Sanctification, which at that time lay in a theological fog.

Many years later Moore emphasized strongly that Keswick

"took its rise, not in a straining after novel interpretations of the Word, but in a deep work of God in individual hearts and lives." No one had hit upon a doctrine which then he sought to apply; it was the other way around. Each leader knew that at some date since 1873 his Christian life had been revolutionized, undoubtedly by the Holy Spirit, and each was groping to define in Scriptural terms what had happened. They used various phrases such as "The Rest of Faith," "the Blessing," "Holiness by Faith," "The Overcoming Life," but every phrase had limits and weakness.

In the heightened tensions of the 1880s, with Holiness preached in varying guises, true and false, it was essential that Keswick think through, or disappear over the precipice. Hopkins was called a theologian by his friends but had no formal theological training. Nor had Webb-Peploe, clear-minded and clear-speaking, yet not a thinker or a writer.

Unless a theologian of first-class caliber joined the movement it might either fizzle out or explode into heresy.

***

Handley Carr Glyn Moule, Principal since 1881 of the new Theological College of Ridley Hall at Cambridge, afterwards Norrisian Professor of Divinity, and for nearly nineteen years Bishop of Durham, was "a recognized theologian of unquestioned Evangelical principles."

In early 1883 he had just passed his forty-first birthday. Dark wavy hair, a prominent nose and full lips gave him rather an un-English look, his ancestry—half-Huguenot, half-Welsh—being perhaps also responsible for the fact that "I was naturally a restless and impatient and somewhat nerveful being." He had taken an important part in D. L. Moody's epochal mission to the University the previous November, and the unprecedented effect of Moody and Sankey lay fresh in memory when Evan Hopkins, Webb-Peploe, Charles Fox and E. W. Moore conducted a Holiness convention at Cambridge.

Moule had understood from hearsay that this teaching "lacked balance" and "had a dangerous drift." He was impressed by the "grave and reverent" manner of "the godly visitors," especially by Webb-Peploe's consideration for his misgivings and Fox's charming courtesy, nor could he deny evidence of blessing among undergraduates. The following year, however, two extremists called Smyth-Pigott and Oliphant, both at that time Anglican curates, held a Holiness mission with "wildish hymns" and the unabashed claim that sin could be eradicated from the believer. They branded Keswick as faithlessly lukewarm—but to Moule they seemed proof of his fears.

His puzzlement grew: "Cambridge was moved in an extraordinary measure and manner by the deepest inquiries and aspirations. The watchwords of surrender and holiness were everywhere. There was an almost passionate desire for entire deliverance from the power of sin. . . . Many an anxious hour some of us had to spend in seeking to guide men, and to indicate the law of balance and holy soberness."

At Easter 1884 appeared Hopkins' book *The Law of Liberty in the Spiritual Life*. During the summer Moule wrote for the *Record* four long anonymous articles on "the contemporary stir of thought, discussion and aspiration upon the great theme of Holiness," in which, having briefly trounced books by extremists, he reviewed exhaustively Evan

Hopkins' "singularly careful treatise" with "sincere respect, but with sometimes stringent criticism." Moule veiled neither admiration for the book's tone nor his uncompromising verdict that its doctrines lacked proportion, were faulty in exegesis and unsound in conclusion. A certain wistfulness crept into these articles. Moule's diary of those summer months records a pathetic catalogue of depression relieved by fitful "hope and peace and gladness." He had "begun to feel, after my years of converted life and ministerial work, guilty of discreditable failure in patience and charity and humbleness, and I know not what."

In September 1884 Moule and his wife and their two little girls went to stay in Scotland with relatives, the Livingstone Learmonths at Park Hall, a country house near Polmont, south of the Forth. Livingstone Learmonth, reputed the handsomest man in his county, had made a fortune sheep farming in Australia. After attending the Keswick of 1882 he had founded for neighbors and friends an annual convention in a great barn on his estate. To Moule's annoyance the convention came around in the course of their visit and there was no escape "without breach of courtesy."

A disgruntled Moule sat at the back of the barn, genuinely afraid that he would be party to heresy, "but there was a great deal of mixed motive, of jealousy and prejudice in it too." The first evening hardened his antipathy, for although Bowker was chairman the host's opening speakers would not have been heard at Keswick! Moule very nearly refused to attend next evening. Courtesy alone drove him to enter the barn again. "God be thanked that I did."

The two addresses Moule heard that night formed together a fair example of the Keswick tone and sequence.

William Sloan, a Glasgow shipowner, "calm, perfectly sane in statement, kind, yet with a rare searching power, spoke of the blight shed on Christian life and work by the failure of the worker to 'put the Lord first' in all things. And the expository picture showed me to myself (under light from above) in a way and degree even agonizing in its force." It "pulled me to pieces," Moule said. It faced him with "the sins of my converted life and its tremendous secret and open failures."

Evan Hopkins stepped to the rostrum unaware that his anonymous *Record* critic sat below—broken, hungry of soul. Hopkins' simple, luminous address "was one long, ordered piling up of the promises of God" to a soul in Handley Moule's sorry case, encouraging him "to expect large and deep deliverances from himself, on the simple condition of surrender into the most trustworthy and tender hands, the hands of a perfect Redeemer, Conqueror, Keeper, and indwelling Friend."

Moule was honest. "And so I listened, and so I yielded, and believed."

In response to Hopkins' closing call Moule stood, "a helpful act of *definition*." To his wonder, his wife stood too. As he walked back to the house, took his lamp and mounted to bed, "I was wonderingly conscious of being in the grasp of an absolute Master, and of having grasped, in Him, a supreme secret of peace and life and victory."

The next night, "My darling and I both publicly confessed blessing; a *blessed* trial. . . . What, *I* delighting in a *convention*?"

Hopkins and Moule borrowed horses from their host and went for two long rides talking Holiness. They became boon companions: "Your once-prejudiced and now most thankful convert and friend," Moule signed himself in a letter of 1889.

Back at Cambridge in October 1884, starting "a very difficult and laborious and perplexing term," Moule found that "by a power not my own I could meet every threatened difficulty with a quiet mind, which was half the victory beforehand"; constant interruptions no longer sprung the "old thrill and twist of impatience," and he told a friend that he had at last learned "to trust God in prayer and to expect definite answers." In November the *Record* printed a letter signed "The writer of Four Papers on Holiness," in which, while not withdrawing his doctrinal position or his criticism of lack of proportion, he freely admitted misreading Hopkins' real meaning, and stated he would be eternally grateful for having now heard and met him.

Moule repaid his debt in the very best way: by preparing a set of scholarly lectures which were delivered to packed audiences of undergraduates and dons in St. Botolph's Church, and later widely circulated in England and abroad as *Thoughts on Christian Sanctity*.

The next years at Cambridge were a microcosm of the atmosphere in Britain. The spiritual tide continued to rise, for this was the time of the Cambridge Seven—that young band of birth and wealth and athletic prowess, whose going out as missionaries to China early in 1885 caught the imagination of the nation and profoundly moved universities. C. T. Studd and Stanley Smith, the leaders, both had experienced crises of consecration and enduement of power. The Seven brought their own alma mater and its Cambridge Inter-Collegiate Christian Union (CICCU) to a peak of evangelistic zeal. Hard on their heels came the unstable Smyth-Pigott, temporarily a Salvation Army officer, to inflame undergraduates with the mental intoxication of the "clean heart"; but already the influence of Moule's lectures, heard and read in all their calm theology, somewhat weighted the balance.

In June 1886, however, shortly before Moule spoke from the platform at Keswick for the first time, the CICCU organized a convention at Cambridge, inviting Bowker as chairman, E. W. Moore, Moule and others—and also Pigott, temporarily an Anglican reading quietly at his old college before reassuming holy orders; Pigott's influence predominated. Moule heard with anxiety and distress "audible proof" that many earnest undergraduates "believed themselves to be quite free from all internal evil." Charles Harford, Canon Harford-Battersby's youngest son,* was one.

The lead in error came from the President of the CICCU, Douglas Hamilton, a man of remarkable beauty of life whose urge for the highest took a fatal turning, driving him out of saintliness to subjective error and, after he had gone down from Cambridge that summer, over the precipice: he disappeared into the Abode of Love, the minute sect of Agapemonites. When Pigott joined him (permanently) the extrem-

---

* Some decades after Canon Harford-Battersby's death his sons dropped the second barrel of their surname. To avoid confusion I will refer from now on to John, Dundas and Charles *Harford*.

ist wing of Holiness made shipwreck.

Moule and Barton, Vicar of Holy Trinity, spent "long and anxious" hours salvaging young men from the wreckage. Charles Harford was among those who corrected course and sailed forward to lives of Christian usefulness. Others lost faith.

In January 1887 Hopkins, carefully briefed by Moule and Barton, led a further convention, and Cambridge evangelical clergy and dons were "thankful without reserve for the solidly and cautiously Scriptural tone of the addresses, the complete absence of excitement."

In afteryears Moule used to say unhesitatingly that the whole result was "nobly good, and many a day since then I have almost prayed for the aberrations back again for the sake of the wonderful life." That the upshot of the Holiness movement of the eighties, in nation as in one university, was "nobly good" may be ascribed, under God, to Keswick and to Handley Moule. Moreover, with the production of *Thoughts on Christian Sanctity,* the movement matured theologically. Hopkins did not disguise his debt to Moule's adjustment of balance and focus.

It becomes possible at last, with Moule rather than Hopkins as basis, briefly to examine Keswick's doctrinal position.

# Nine

## The Open Secret

"What is meant by 'Keswick teaching'? But this term I abhor. I heartily wish the place had not been identified with the teaching which is given here. We have no new doctrine, no new truth to bring forward. We have only the old evangelical Biblical truth to inculcate." Webb-Peploe's words at a Ministers' Meeting in 1890 would have been echoed by other early leaders of "What is sometimes called 'The Keswick Movement,'" another term which, Webb-Peploe said, "is a false and unmeaning one really, for the Movement was nothing less than the gracious working of the Holy Spirit."

Speakers from the Keswick platform were not clamped to a party line. They signed no statement of doctrine. Bishop Moule did not hesitate to admit towards the end of his life, "Keswick has not always seen all of its people so true to its true message as never to invite a legitimate anxiety." He affirmed, and all veterans would have affirmed with him, the wholesomeness, soundness and nobility of the general rule, the weight of doctrine and influence.

"Keswick stands," Bishop Moule could say, "for the great and eternal truths, some of which, so to speak, it takes for granted but never forgets: the glory of our Lord Jesus Christ. . . . His death for us upon the Cross: Keswick is firm as a rock upon the sacrifice of the death of Christ, and the benefit of pardon, utterly unmerited by us, which we have because Jesus died." Accepting and deriving from the basic facts of the Christian faith and the authority of the Bible, Keswick brought "into new prominence an all too much forgotten truth of the gospel." The Holiness movement did not originate, but recovered, an "oft-forgotten, oft-misunderstood, oft-misapplied but blessed and living truth."

In his *Thoughts on Christian Sanctity* Moule has a fine passage on the aim of Christians who genuinely desire sanctity: "To be like [Christ]. To displace self from the inner throne and to enthrone Him; to make not the slightest compromise with the smallest sin. We aim at nothing less than to walk with God all day long, to abide every hour in Christ, and He and His words in us, to love God with all the heart, and our neighbor as ourselves." Moule makes the stupendous claim that "it is possible to cast every care on Him daily, and to be at peace amidst pressure, to see the will of God in everything, to put away *all* bitterness and clamor and evil speaking, daily and hourly. It is possible by unreserved resort to divine power under divine conditions to become strongest through and through at our weakest point."

The vital question concerns not the aim of sanctity but the means. When Keswick speakers contrasted the possibilities with the characteristics of the average contemporary Christian, they did not differ from ten thousand preachers in ten thousand churches, except perhaps in the frankness of detailed diagnosis. The difference lay in therapy.

"Was not the old Evangelical teaching," Webb-Peploe once suggested, "something like this: that I was perfectly justified in a moment and had then a standing before God; then at that moment sanctification commenced and I had to go on, struggle and strive, and call in the aid of the Holy Ghost, which one too often forgot to do. I was to struggle, and the Holy Ghost would aid me. . . . I was continually expecting defeat, and if I conquered I thought it wonderful."

Against this Keswick set the truth of Christ the Victor.

"It does not depend on wearisome struggle," says Moule, "but on God's power to take the consecrated soul and to keep him. God is an eternal Person undertaking for you." "Keswick stands distinctively for this: Christ our righteousness, upon Calvary, received by faith, is also Christ our holiness, in the heart that submits to Him and relies upon Him. . . . A message as old as the Apostles but too much forgotten: the open secret of inward victory for liberty in life and service through the trusted power of an indwelling Christ; Christ in us for our deliverance from sin, for our emancipation from the tyranny of self, for the conquest of temptation."

The entrance is a twin door: surrender and faith.

"Would we know the Christ *in us* in His power? We must yield ourselves to the Christ *over us*, in His will, His rights. This great truth of Christ over us by every claim of lordship, sovereignty and possession is the other side of Keswick's distinctive message." When Moule, a distinguished classicist as well as theologian, had been walking back from the barn at Park Hall that night in September 1884, there floated into his mind Aristotle's definition of a slave: "a chattel that lives." Henceforth Moule was a slave of Christ, and it was a metaphor he loved to dwell upon: "My Master, my Possessor; absolute, not constitutional, supremely entitled to order me about all day. How delightful the thought that hands or head or voice are indeed the implements of the faithful slave, kept at work for such an owner—His property, and glad indeed to be so."

In his lectures Moule elaborated this theme in the context of church and individual, of work, play, holidays, and of deliberate vocation, and pointed out that Christ's slave, unlike Aristotle's, may understand his Master's will and, moreover, at any time may desert; therefore his slavery is perfect freedom. The relationship is one of intimate friendship: "His slave who is also His friend. . . . I would not for a moment be free, an independent agent, choosing work and bargaining for pay. I have no rights, I make no conditions. I am a 'chattel that lives.' But ah! with it, and in it, and through it, I am my Master's friend."

Thus, in surrender comes faith, the certainty that the Master's interest is to provide his slave's every need—physical, moral, mental and spiritual. "As the soul trusts Him, and entrusts itself to Him, so shall He have His way and do His work and, at the very springs of thought and will, put out His blessed loving power, fulfilling the promise, 'I will subdue their iniquities, I will write My laws in their hearts, and put them in their minds.'"

---

Keswick acted on the belief that many listeners would yield and trust in an instant; the Convention's course was directed to that end and a silent "act of definition" encouraged. This had its dangers.

"In those early days," wrote Hubert Brooke, "there were many testimonies of a practical deliverance from the power of besetting sin, a constant and lasting blessing found in the keeping power of Christ, which formed so new and blessed an experience that many spoke of it as a 'second conversion.' Though that phase was never adopted by the speakers, nor given any official approval, yet it was one quite natural under the circumstances." Moule uttered a strong warning (in 1890): "There is a risk, when it is too much insisted upon, that an instantaneous experience of a liberty unknown before is an essential." A crisis, he said, might be the beginning of this deeper spiritual life for many, but not for all; and to claim that it could begin only at a convention was absurd.

Even more emphatically, Keswick guarded against the suggestion that the act of surrender and faith on the part of a true Christian meant the creation of a "clean heart" spiritually different from the new nature which had been his since the moment he was born again; or meant the total disappearance of what Paul called "the flesh" or "the old man." "Keswick has rejected," wrote the biographer of Hopkins, summing up his teaching, "the doctrine of *eradication*, as though the soul, 'empty swept and garnished,' were secure now from contamination and incapable of defilement; and has insisted on the wiser doctrine and happier experience of *counter-action*, in which the soul is delivered, and kept, and led from strength to strength only through the grace and mightiness of One who dwells within it, a sin-restraining and sin-conquering Saviour." Conversely, it is still possible to lapse: "We know ourselves," wrote Moule, "to be always and everywhere poor sinners, carrying the 'carnal mind' very really in our constitution, ready to assert all its tyranny when a man neglects to use the glorious promise and presence of the Holy Ghost."

Finally, this full surrender is a beginning, not an end. Sanctification is not complete in an instant, but should progress, cultivated by prayer, study of the Scriptures, worship and the Breaking of Bread. Discipline and effort are not redundant, but of different quality, and for a different purpose: not self-centered climbing towards blessedness, but vital accessories of the service which is perfect freedom. "'Present your bodies,' quoted Hubert Brooke, 'a living sacrifice, holy, acceptable unto God, which is your reasonable service.' These two thoughts formed the right and left hand of the subject: cleansing and consecration, deliverance and dedication." Moule adds: "The inmost secret of deliverance and purification, behind all 'means,' is faith; watchful and submissive reliance in the power of the indwelling and also exalted Lord."

Here, then, in brief lay the kernel, "Christ in us, Christ over us," of the teaching heard at Keswick, to be developed and expounded and illustrated and tested by the whole range of Holy Scripture and human context.

Thirty-one years after his Park Hall experience and four before he died, Bishop Moule looked back, and his words fitly express the attitude of the makers of Keswick to their message: "God knows how imperfectly I have used my secret. I repent before Him in great humiliation. But I know the secret, His open secret of victory and rest. And I know how different life has been for that secret."

The deeper definition of the doctrines of Sanctification and the Holy Spirit which followed the accession of Moule did not, as yet, lead to over-systematizing. Sometimes speakers went a little too deep. "I do hope," murmured Robert Wilson, looking at Hopkins and Moule keyed up to address the Tent, "these two dear brethren will feed the *lambs* tonight." Old Haslam, after the Convention of 1889, overheard the remark: "People get teaching at the Tent but their blessing at the Salvation Army."

Any overemphasis on solid doctrine was a small price to pay for firm theological foundations. When a last storm of criticism blew up in 1890 it was Moule who stilled it, in letters to the *Record* notable not only for learning but for a loving kindness and a humility missing so often from nineteenth-century theological dispute. Thenceforth Keswick stood accepted by British evangelicals, whether or not actively cooperating, a fact symbolized by the appearance on the platform in 1892, on the Sunday following the close of the Convention proper, of that foremost past critic, Bishop Ryle of Liverpool. He offered prayer and "listened with evident satisfaction"; this was not surprising, for the Chairman tactfully had invited D. L. Moody, who had attended the last part of the week as a listener, to give the address.*

---

* D. L. Moody, as will be seen, became a strong supporter although not able to attend again. Ryle did not reappear. Ryle (not then a bishop) had in fact preached at St. John's on the Sunday previous to the Convention of 1879, but this must have been from respect and friendship for Harford-Battersby; he did not stay for meetings in the Tent.

"You have not gathered merely for your own soul comfort and enjoyment. If you think only of that, any 'blessing' you may receive will be very fleeting." Webb-Peploe's words at the Convention of 1884 sum up a strong and constant emphasis.

That the outworking of holiness should be "a homely and practical thing in the warp and woof of life" was neatly demonstrated by a famous remark of Webb-Peploe's the next year, 1885: "No doubt you all think yourselves consecrated people, but let me remind you of what you are going to do tonight. You are going to put outside your bedroom doors two thousand pairs of dirty boots, and you expect them all clean and shining by half-past six tomorrow morning, that you may come to the early prayer meeting. And how much do you think of the 'slaveys' who will have to do it?" Moule defined holiness as a "right character going out into right conduct all round," and there is little doubt that the influence of Keswick did much to sweeten Christian behavior in the later nineteenth century.

Holiness can never be an end in itself. From earliest days the Conventions had evangelistic outreach to people and visitors to the town. On each Saturday evening, before and after, the Tent held a special service; open-air meetings already were arranged in the Market Place, and there was a time when every court and alley had visits every year, an activity significant of the Christian dedication and energy scattered to the four corners of the land as each Convention ended. Keswick from the first had yet another outreach in its contribution to the unity of Christians.

Then, when theological foundations had been secured and the first decade surmounted, "there sprang up before the

Convention," in Brooke's words, "quite unexpectedly and without human design, the great vista of an unevangelized world."

# Ten

---

# The Irresistible Claim

A spiritual deepening could engender willingness to serve overseas. "I would even go so far as to say that had I never gone to Keswick I might never have been a missionary," wrote Alfred Tucker, the lion-shooting, tribal warfare quelling, tough pioneering Bishop of Uganda. But Tucker, a Lakeland artist renowned for having in twenty-four hours walked sixty miles climbing Scafell, Bow Fell, Skiddaw and Helvellyn, did not offer for Africa until years after his first attendance at Keswick in 1876. His story is typical of the unobtrusive leavening in the early Conventions.

This leavening received no official encouragement. When asked to include a missionary meeting Bowker would reply: "No! Missions mean secretaries quarreling for collections. It would spoil Keswick."

He was not unfriendly; Bowker and his colleagues rejoiced that "many young men who are now actively engaged in distant lands can date their 'special call' to this service from solemn seasons of personal consecration at Keswick."

It was not the negative approach of the convener of the Perth Conference many years before who crushed the young Hudson Taylor wanting to appeal for China with the remark: "My dear sir, surely you mistake the character of the Conference. These meetings are for *spiritual edification!*" Little Hudson Taylor, the timid yet courageous founder of the interdenominational China Inland Mission, now a man of fifty-one, his sandy hair nearly grey, came to the Convention of 1883. He had long believed that the way to find men and women for overseas is to deepen the life of the home churches, and in 1869—brought by years of hardship, disappointment and persecution in China to despair—he had discovered overwhelmingly the reality of the "Exchanged Life," "Not I but Christ." Keswick seemed to Hudson Taylor a tremendous potential for the whole missionary cause, and he soon referred to it as "my happy hunting ground."

The official attitude remained rigid. At the Convention of 1885, the summer following the Cambridge Seven, an elderly Liverpool solicitor called Reginald Radcliffe, a prominent lay evangelist who had awakened to the missionary claim only in his latter years, approached Bowker and once more was refused a missionary meeting. Radcliffe invited a few of his friends, young and old, to join him for a private missionary prayer meeting in his lodgings in Station Road, "a house with oriel windows." Eugene Stock came, the renowned lay-secretary of the Church Missionary Society—at Keswick for the first time; and Barclay Buxton, Webb-Peploe's new-fledged curate, future founder of the Japan Evangelistic Band; and Archibald Orr-Ewing, a Dumbartonshire dye manufacturer, just twenty-eight, who later spent a quarter-century with the C.I.M. in China. "It was expected that a *few* friends would gather," recalls Walter B. Sloan, son of the Sloan whom Moule had heard at Park Hall, "but they came until the room was so crowded that we could not even kneel in prayer—we had to stand; and there were still people on the stairs wanting to get in. The cry of the hearts of God's servants was that He would lead us out to tell the world of its need, and that he would move here in Keswick to send forth blessing throughout the earth."

At the Testimony Meeting on the Friday afternoon (in those years people in the body of the Tent might rise in their places for a sentence or two) the testimonies were following their normal course when, notes Stock, "a bright-looking young Cambridge undergraduate got up and with beaming face" said that although he had known the Cambridge Seven personally he had felt no call to the foreign field until some incidental words from Fox the previous evening "conveyed God's call to go abroad irresistibly." Charles Harford sprang up and expressed joy at his fellow-undergraduate's decision. Suddenly three young Cambridge clergymen stood together and announced their willingness to serve overseas. "The effect on the assembly was indescribable."*

The next year Bowker allowed Radcliffe to use the Tent for a missionary meeting "unconnected with the Convention," on the Saturday morning which those remaining after the official close (the 7 a.m. Thanksgiving) devoted to ex-

---

* One, C. H. Hope-Gill, went to India shortly and eventually became Bishop of Travancore and Cochin. For twenty-two years it seemed he would be the sole missionary of the trio, until in 1907 Canon Gerald Lander of Liverpool was consecrated Bishop of Victoria, Hong Kong. As a Trinity undergraduate Lander had tried to wreck Moody's mission and was converted after calling to apologize.

cursions. Bowker ostentatiously absented himself: Webb-Peploe, a Committee member of C.M.S., instead of leading his usual party of walking enthusiasts to the summit of Scafell Pike (to Borrowdale by dog-cart except for energetic undergraduates with penny-farthings, then up past Styhead tarn) took a place on the platform.

1887 saw the break. A missionary had written from Palestine to ask Bowker if he would appeal for ten ladies who could go out at their own expense under C.M.S. Bowker read out the letter.

Its definite call crystalized an awareness which had been growing daily. The morning Ladies Meetings in the Lecture Hall were already strongly mission minded; the Convention of '87 had drawn more young men than ever before, many searching where to commit their futures; the C.M.S. had a mixed houseparty of members on furlough from Africa and the East; and Hudson Taylor back again from China was unselfishly promoting the interests of all continents. To a young Scot, Dan Crawford, who bewailed his fear of isolation and loneliness if he obeyed an urge towards inland Africa, saying, "The Devil will shut me in," Taylor instantly replied: "Yes, but he can't *roof* you in." Crawford worked twenty-two years without a break "in the long grass of Central Africa."

Bowker again lent the Tent for Saturday morning and removed himself. Nearly every seat taken, "the missionary meeting was one of the brightest and best of all the week, and its three hours were all too short." Radcliffe took the chair. Taylor opened, followed by Stock, Webb-Peploe, a West African negro clergyman called James Johnson, afterwards a bishop, and three women on the eve of sailing. "It was a thrilling sight, runs a contemporary account, "to see the large band of missionaries present . . . but still more thrilling to see the yet larger band who stood, as ready now to go, and a third band whose hearts were ready but with no plans formed."

In his address Stock had invited those wanting information about missionary service to come to his lodgings and he would direct them to any society or mission. "What was the result? Between three o'clock that Saturday and nine o'clock on Monday night I had twenty-four long private interviews. . . . I wrote and told Bowker, and he replied appreciatively, but would not infringe his principle, 'No Missions at Keswick'!"

Sunday, Monday and Tuesday, Radcliffe used the Tent to stoke the fires among those hundreds who, in that leisured age, were in no hurry to leave Keswick. Meanwhile, Webb-Peploe and Johnson traveled to London, and on the Tuesday reported to the C.M.S. Committee. "A solemn impression was produced, and earnest prayer was offered that God would guide what might possibly turn out to be an important missionary impulse." That autumn the C.M.S. made a memorable decision of faith: to refuse no suitable candidate, to keep back no missionary ready to sail, on financial grounds alone.

The following May, 1888, Stock received a letter from Bowker, his close friend, which must have amused as well as heartened Hudson Taylor if he saw it before leaving England that June. Bowker wrote that "a new thought has been given me: Consecration and the Evangelization of the world ought to go together."

Bowker's change of direction proved thorough. When Stock reached Keswick in the rain (1888 being one of the wettest Conventions), Bowker told him that the missionary meeting on Saturday would be officially sponsored; there would be another on Wednesday, and that, in the absence of Reginald Radcliffe in America, Stock should arrange both. "I was surprised, and hesitated, but on pressure agreed, on the condition that I might also have a short, daily missionary prayer meeting. The expediency of this was doubted but I was allowed to have it," twenty minutes in the Drill Hall, "squeezed in between the other morning gatherings," but highly attended from the start.

Eugene Stock, then fifty-two, was a man of broad culture and common sense. Bowker's choice could not have been better. Stock did not ask famous leaders to deliver long addresses, which would have killed the meetings. He selected a large number of missionaries on furlough, and recruits ready to sail, told them that this was no time for the ordinary run of anecdote and information—no mention of an individual society, no word of money—each must set forth in brief (some spoke ten minutes, some two), and warm from personal experience, "the claim of Christ to His people's willing service in the cause of the evangelization of the world."

The three hours that wet Saturday morning, July 28, 1888, graced by Bowker as chairman, Wilson and their colleagues, seemed "the shortest of all the Keswick meetings," though longest. Stock's brilliant scheme has ensured that year after year the hours (subsequently reduced to two) would fly unobserved by an audience gripped in the projection of the world's need and the Great Commission through a succession of brief statements, vivid and contemporary.

Stock had uttered a warning that "the question to be asked is not merely, 'Lord, what wilt Thou have me to do?'

but 'Lord, where wilt Thou have me to do it?'. . . . Readiness to go out must be accompanied with readiness to stop at home if the Lord so orders it." Stock knew the danger of vocation grounded on emotional response to appeal; knew too that once offers were made, responsible authorities would sift and train. The key was willingness.

In the middle of the meeting occurred a trivial incident with vast result.

A young man in the audience handed an envelope to a steward—so quietly that no one ever discovered who he was, except Stock, who divulged no further description than "a Cambridge undergraduate." The steward took up the envelope to Bowker who found inside a large, crisp, white bank note for the then considerable sum of £10, folded around an anonymous message. He read it out during a pause in the proceedings: "This £10, my savings for the year, I was going to put into the savings bank, but feeling the Lord wants it, I hand it in as a thank offering for blessing received in the Convention, to be used, if others will join, to send out a 'Keswick Missionary.'" Bowker made no comment.

No collection would be taken at the missionary meeting. Bowker had made that plain.

Charles Fox gave a closing address. In silence, scores rose to signify willingness to serve wherever God should send. Bowker announced the final hymn. The Tent was ringing with the strains of *All Hail the Power of Jesus' Name*, to the tune *Miles Lane*, when people noticed slips of paper being sent up to the platform. Consequently the audience did not disperse, curious at the growing pile on the chairman's desk. Bowker opened envelopes: "Another ten promised!" . . . "Another ten!" . . . "Another ten!" Slips were soon being sent as fast as stewards could collect—the Tent astir with bits of paper and the movement of pencils as promises were scribbled surreptitiously under cover of hymn books or Bibles.

"£25 a year!" called Bowker, unfolding another paper. . . . "Two offers of £100 each!" A voice called out: "Praise God from whom all blessings flow," and the whole Tent sang the doxology.

Old Bowker, perhaps murmuring a despairing "Missions mean secretaries quarreling for collections," carried from the platform promises and bank notes which were found to total £860. This grew before the end of the year to £1060 1s. 8d., a small proportion being designated for individual missions, leaving at the disposal of the Convention no less than £908 8s. 8d., including the original £10 note.*

——— ——— ———

The events of 1888 gave the missionary factor a firm, and in some years a dominant, place in Conventions of the future, and to Keswick a special importance for overseas missions.

The establishment of a Hospitality Fund in 1889 enabled missionaries on furlough to attend, thus increasing the number of men and women who gained strength and inspiration before returning to the field—C.M.S., C.I.M., and the Zenana missions being the earliest to realize Keswick's value.

Two incidents were typical of many. On the Friday of

---

* For comparison, £908 per annum in 1888 would be a comfortable income for a professional man with a family.

the 1890 Convention the Handley Moules arranged a little excursion of C.M.S. missionaries to the Lodore Falls. Sitting around in a field after their picnic, they were invited by Moule to say a few words on what the Convention had meant, whereupon Joseph Hoare of Ningpo, mid-China, "the last man to be affected by anything that could be called a 'gushing' influence, spoke in quiet and restrained language of the blessing he had received." At the Saturday meeting, when the slips of paper went up (the custom continued for some years), his slip announced, anonymously, that he and his wife would henceforth serve at their own expense. He became Bishop of Victoria, Hong Kong, and was drowned in the typhoon of 1906.

Another Joseph, Joseph Hill, came to Keswick a year or two later, newly consecrated Bishop of Western Equatorial Africa, from New Zealand. At the Ministers' Meeting, Webb-Peploe spoke of the prophet Ezekiel's obedience when his wife had died suddenly and he had been told, "neither shalt thou mourn nor weep," as an instance of "willingness to go to the uttermost with God." Bishop Hill jumped up and, recalls another minister present, "with tears on his cheeks said he could go a long way, but he could not go as far as that. But Webb-Peploe assured him that God would never ask him to suffer anything for which He would not supply sufficient grace. Bishop Hill need not have bothered, for when the call came (in Nigeria) he was in one room and his wife was in another room, and they neither of them knew the other was gone till they met up in Glory." They had landed at Lagos, caught yellow fever three weeks later, were put in separate rooms and died in a few hours, he during the afternoon, she at midnight.

Keswick influenced mission policy too.

Half a dozen prominent C.M.S. men, hitherto, aloof attended the Convention of 1890. On the fourth day they asked Webb-Peploe, Moule, Brooke and several others to join them in private discussion, from which emerged a letter sent at once to London. This "Keswick Letter" urged the Society that the worldwide need of the hour "is so startling that it justifies an advance on a wide scale under the directing hand of God." One thousand missionaries should be appealed for, of highest spiritual caliber. The C.M.S. responded warmly. Critics complained that it was dreadful to see the C.M.S. follow Keswick, until the Archbishop of Canterbury (Benson) silenced them by saying, "I am thankful for that Meeting which lifted up its voice and said suddenly, 'You must send out a thousand more.'" He quoted the old football cry, *Follow up!* "Follow up," he said, "or you will not win the goal."

Keswick itself certainly followed up the victory of 1888. Every year the main missionary meeting would be reinforced by others unofficial. Macartney, over again from Australia in 1893, from the slopes of Skiddaw one afternoon "looked down on a great fleet of seventy boats returning" from a missionary picnic on St. Hubert's Island; Friars Crag saw gatherings to introduce "heroes and heroines of the foreign field . . . all utterly unlike our original conception." At the Drill Hall Eugene Stock organized "a grand review of the 'Missionary Army,'" ranging them first by societies, then by countries. Already national Christians were welcomed, although, in the 1890s, a brown or black or yellow face would still inevitably be conspicuous.

But what of the £10 note and its fellows?

# Eleven

## Wide Horizons

A fund raised in Canon Harford-Battersby's memory had been used to buy out his part-ownership of the Eskin Street plot, and Wilson deeded his own share to the Keswick Trust consequently established. The "Keswick Trustees," Wilson, Bowker and John Harford, were the only persons with any legal standing in the affairs of the Convention, their duties as Trustees being confined to the Trust's holding of land, Tent and furnishings, and the expenses fund raised annually by the collections; Convention arrangements remained informally in the hands of Wilson and Bowker as private individuals.

On the arrival of the £10 note and the rest of the £908 8s. 8d. at the absolute disposal of the Convention, "the Trustees were perplexed," writes Stock, "what to do with the money. It looked at first as if Bowker's fears about secretaries and collections might be justified."

Bowker called a meeting at his home in St. John's Wood near Lord's Cricket Ground on November 29, 1888, to which he invited his two fellow Trustees and Hopkins, Webb-Peploe, Fox, E. W. Moore, Hubert Brooke and Eugene Stock. Stock suggested that "as the 'Keswick message' was a message not to the heathen but to Christians, they should use the money to send out, not missionaries but *missioners*, to hold special services in Christian congregations in the Colonies and in the mission field." Stock's brilliant idea did not spring from a vacuum; the C.M.S. had recently begun the practice of sending clergymen from home on short tours for such a purpose, first to West Africa and then to India, in the cold seasons. Stock put forward the name of one of them as a possible "Keswick Missioner": young George Grubb, a slightly eccentric, enormously tall Irishman.

They debated again at Easter time, 1889, at a country house near Stroud in Gloucestershire, and confirmed Grubb's appointment. They discussed a further plan which might have had unfortunate results: "a pioneer mission in China, in districts not yet evangelized. . . . The desire being rather to send out evangelists, two and two, to proclaim the gospel, than to establish fresh mission stations and churches." It would be chiefly "a lay agency, on undenominational lines," the converts to be told to connect themselves with the nearest evangelical mission.

Apart from the awkwardness—unperceived in the placid purlieus of Stroud—that a convert's nearest mission might be two or three weeks' walk, the informal committee should have inferred that such a scheme must develop into a separate Keswick Missionary Society or denomination, whatever their intentions to the contrary. When friends of Moody planned a similar organization based on the Northfield Conference, Moody promptly crushed it; the Keswick speakers dabbled with their scheme for over eighteen months. Finally they settled upon the admirable alternative of regular grants to a small number, new or established, who were thoroughly in sympathy with the Convention, working as ordinary members of a recognized body, but to be known as "Keswick Missionaries." The first to receive a Keswick grant (though not the first to be termed a Keswick Missionary) became the best known: Amy Carmichael, who had lived at Broughton Grange as the widowed Robert Wilson's adopted daughter since the age of twenty-two, her subsequent awareness of a missionary call bringing one of the sharpest sacrifices of his life: his heart was breaking as he presented her to the Keswick Mission Committee during the Convention of 1892. She served first in Japan under Barclay Buxton, then in Ceylon before beginning the work that led to the founding of the Dohnavur Fellowship in South India, her fame as "Amma," and her books and verse.

George Grubb and his party sailed for Ceylon on October 17, 1889, five weeks after the death of Bowker, who had gallantly taken the chair at the previous Convention, though broken in health and obliged to have others speak for him.

George Carleton Grubb from Tipperary, then aged thirty-three, was an extraordinary character. Everything about him had a rip-roaring wild Irishness. He would have an audience cringing in fear of judgment one moment and bursting their sides with guffaws the next. "Please don't put Grubb before a solemn closing meeting. He is too jocular," Hopkins begged Wilson before one Convention. Grubb was a man of emotions, not happy unless in strong measure he could feel the presence of God, but a man of sheer faith who fully expected, and often saw, the most improbable occurrences in answer to prayer. His views were black and white. He dismissed all culture as worldly. He could be intolerant to a degree; yet such was the breadth of his influence that the extreme High Church bishop of Cape Town had him cross the oceans to conduct a mission in cathedral and diocese, while the Salvation Army counted him almost one of themselves! "He was a joyous person," writes his nephew, Sir Kenneth Grubb, "infectious in his happiness and his enthusiasm. He had a gift for making people of all ages, young as well as old, feel at home in his company. If he said hard things in his preaching he said them in such form that offense could not reasonably be taken. More often, however, whether in his private conversations or in his public work, he would impress everyone as a man to whom Christ our *life* was a vital and personal reality. His prayers in his private circle were three parts praise and thanksgiving. He always rejoiced in God."

Grubb's forthright hot-gospeling penetrated where delicate persuasions fell short. His power among fast-living young Englishmen in distant edges of the Empire may be deduced from the record of the party's arrival in Colombo: "We had no sooner made fast when a company of saved tea-planters came on board to welcome us, especially their old friend Mr. Grubb, through whom so many had received blessing during his previous mission. These dear fellows are out-and-out, which makes one jump for joy that they are not ashamed to fly the banner of love. They simply seized us and took us ashore, there being two boats ready. We sang lustily, praising God for all His goodness both to the dear fellows in their tea gardens and to us on board ship."

The writer of this exuberant record was twenty-seven-year-old Edward Candlish Millard, who sailed as manager to the hopelessly impracticable Grubb. Millard had been a tea taster in Shanghai and London, then devoted himself fulltime to a rapidly expanding lay ministry only to find invitations dry up. His funds dried up too. He refused a temptingly lucrative offer to return to tea, certain he had not mistaken his call. He offered for Keswick's abortive China mission; at the '89 Convention, Grubb invited him.

Grubb, his nephew Richardson, Millard, a third young man called Walter Campbell, and a Tamil evangelist, David, stayed in Ceylon until opportunities were exhausted and then crossed to South India with unflagging gusto and undisputed spiritual success among planters, missionaries, and national Christians. Impartial evidence bears out what Millard wrote in March 1890: "The missionaries, wherever we go, say they are sure this 'Mission to Missions' is the plan that the Lord is indirectly blessing to the heathen, for they themselves get greatly cheered, and many native Christians are led to grasp the promises offered through faith in Jesus, and the many consecrations of the converted will spread to the heathen daily."

The four Britons left for the Antipodes by steamer in company of "three Roman Catholic priests (French), two C.M.S. missionaries, one Methodist, two Congregational ministers, six professional jockeys, a theatrical troupe, two horse dealers, an old infidel lecturer, a Jew, some gold diggers, several families and about thirty children." At Melbourne, Grubb was persuaded by H. B. Macartney to stop for a fortnight's mission, rejoining the others in New Zealand where they held missions for three months, mostly in Anglican parishes, until they set off for South Africa (in response to the High Church bishop) by what they had discovered to be the quickest route: Honolulu, San Francisco, New York, Queenstown —and Keswick, which they reached hotfoot and unexpected in the middle of the Convention, creating an immense sensation, except to a couple of old ladies who had prayed to that effect, though whether after studying the steamer schedules is not revealed.

After returning from South Africa at the end of 1890 Grubb and Millard were off again, with Millard's bride, to Australia in April 1891. Walter Campbell meanwhile had accompanied the venerable Haslam for a six months' Keswick mission to India, a most acceptable, if less acrobatic, venture.

George Grubb's mission to Australia and New Zealand, 1891–92, proved even more spectacular than the first. Keswick had to pay only a small proportion of the expenses because Australians and New Zealanders showered him with gifts and hospitality, and amazing scenes were witnessed at his evangelistic services. Eugene Stock, crossing Grubb's tracks a few months later, wrote back: "Whenever I find myself in parishes where Grubb and the others have labored, there I am sure to find many who are rejoicing in the Lord and proving His power to use them in His service." Stock saw the signs of true revival, in that the effect had not been confined to places visited by Grubb, and added: "Although the direct work has been mainly among English colonists, yet indirectly a mighty missionary work has been done. . . . For the candidates now coming forward in numbers for missionary service are, many of them, though not all, the fruit of Grubb's mission"—a verdict Stock was able to substantiate seven years later in his monumental *History of the Church Missionary Society*.

While Grubb was in Victoria he and Macartney founded near Melbourne the Geelong Convention, "arranged on the lines of the Keswick Convention," in late September 1891. The Grubb influence made the hallelujahs ring; Hopkins or Moule would have blanched—and indeed the Geelong Conventions eventually fell into the hands of extremists and had disappeared before 1918.

One incident at the first Geelong Convention even reached the staid columns of *The Times* of London. At the close of the missionary meeting, before Grubb pronounced the benediction, a woman quietly sent up a slip of paper enclosing £2 for the China Inland Mission. Gifts began to pour. "The people responded," reported *The Times*, "by giving their purses unopened, their watches and rings, while women stripped off their jewelry and personal adornments. Others gave hastily-executed conveyances of land and other property. In a few minutes money and property valued at £1500 had been subscribed." Grubb, in his report at the 1892 Keswick, said there were gold watches enough to need a pony and cart, and "an archdeacon actually put down his archdeaconal ring upon the table, and that archdeacon got his soul united to God in a way that he never knew before, and now he is just as bad as the Grubb lunatics in his own parish—and souls are being saved by him all over the country."

The resounding impression created by the missions of George Grubb convinced the Keswick platform that they had responded correctly to the challenge of the £10 note. Thenceforth, year by year, one or more deputations of the "Keswick Convention Mission" boarded liners at Tilbury or Southampton for South America or China or Canada, the Mediterranean, India. Several of the younger generation coming into prominence took part, while Hopkins and others accepted invitations to conduct conventions in European centers.

And thus, in the 1890s, the name of Keswick became familiar throughout the world. In days when new and disturbing ideas were percolating among missionaries, the arrival of a Keswick missioner or the establishment of a local convention by someone who had attended Keswick during home leave, would strengthen and reassure. "I hear of *great need* among our missy. brethren and sisters," wrote Wilson to Grubb in October 1893, "not in the same way, but not much behind the need of those who know *Him* not. Whether it is better *never* to know, or having known to set aside the atonement and fritter away God's Word, as too many are doing? Then those who do not do this—are often so *powerless* in the face of the Enemy, because they lack the knowledge of the energizing power of the Holy Ghost. Oh, my brother there is a *deep need*. . . ."

To meet that need Wilson and his friends gave time and prayer and labor. From 1890 they arranged for free copies of the *Life of Faith* (which became a weekly in 1892) to be sent overseas, and it was to enable missionaries to share in the Convention that the addresses were bound together for the first time in 1892 as the *Story of Keswick,* and subsequently as the *Keswick Week*; over seventeen hundred free copies were sent abroad that year by the Keswick Mission Fund, a service repeated and enlarged annually. The Fund also gave hospitality to a Convention houseparty for missionaries.

For all these varied activities a collection was taken at the Saturday missionary meeting and on Wednesday afternoons, which became the traditional time for Keswick missioners to report their travels. And behind them, under the palms or in eastern hills, or in the suburbs of thriving young cities of the Colonies, conventions "on Keswick lines" (as the phrase was) were becoming annual features of the Christian year.

# Twelve

## Two Problems

The rise of the Keswick Mission had two important incidental effects on the Convention's history.

In 1895 rumor asserted that George Grubb sometimes taught private inquirers at his missions the doctrine of Conditional Immortality (that only the saved in Christ have existence after the resurrection and judgment, the impenitent being annihilated, suffering no conscious hell)—a doctrine that could not be labeled orthodox, nor, lying in that doctrinal limbo where revelation grants no sharp outlines, as clearly heterodox. The matter lay rather within the scope of private judgment.

Elder Cumming and Webb-Peploe, having confronted Grubb and learned that he deemed this doctrine "so important that he could make no promise to refrain," urged the platform to withdraw him from the Keswick mission which was about to visit Alexandria in Egypt. Wise old Robert Wilson, who since Bowker's death had been chairman of the Convention, took no action. Grubb went to Alexandria.

"It is high time," wrote Webb-Peploe to Wilson the following November, "that the real leaders of Keswick took a determined stand upon some of these heresies which are introduced by the great enemy to rend God's Church. . . . It will be impossible for men like Dr. Moule and myself to identify ourselves with men like Mr. Grubb, however much we love the man, if we desire to have any influence for good in the Church." For Webb-Peploe there was no quibble: Grubb and his friends "distinctly identify themselves with heresies."

Charles Fox did not agree with Grubb and recognized that "It is not what *we* think but what others think, which is the whole matter with Grubb." He counseled, however, "Let us have faith in God and lie low, and keep silent—some greater blessing will soon break then." E. W. Moore, whom Webb-Peploe still tended to tar with a Sinless Perfection brush as another heretic, wrote to Wilson in February 1896: "There is a certain section of speakers on our platform who would narrow down the teaching to their own poverty-stricken views."

Moore put his finger on the crux of the issue. Where should Keswick draw its doctrinal frontier? Should it be exclusive or inclusive, invite only those who held views that no other speaker would ever question, or those who, under the broad roof of evangelical doctrine, were firm on Keswick's central message but might differ, publicly or privately, on other matters?

Grubb went to Canada for Keswick in the spring of 1896. Signs and wonders continued. Wilson wrote to Fox: "If Keswick won't own those whom the Lord does—Grubb, Moore, Gregson,* etc., where are we? High and *very* dry, I

* The Rev. Gelson Gregson, with Grubb in Canada; previous to being a Keswick missioner he had done remarkable work among British soldiers in India.

fear." On the other hand General Hatt Noble, a leading Anglican layman in Keswick counsels, while not considering Grubb a heretic, thought that in attempting to unravel what God had kept hidden, he was "very wrong. . . . Why for such frivolous causes should he wish to bring a root of bitterness and division into Keswick?"

The matter was resolved by a compromise which effectively guarded Keswick both from barren exclusiveness and from becoming a forum for dangerous individualists. A statement was drafted and publicly issued in 1896 "for the guidance of speakers at all Conventions connected with Keswick," declaring that such, "and all missioners sent forth at the instance of the Keswick Convention," would consider themselves "pledged, so far as possible, not to teach during the Convention, or such mission, any doctrines or opinions but those upon which there is general agreement among the promoters of such Conventions."

The shackles of subscription to an exclusive statement of exact definitions were avoided, and the heresy hunting which this could engender. Grubb, however, declined to sign the statement. Without open break, or uttering one word of criticism or hostility, he dropped from the Keswick team and for the next sixteen years worked independently in Australia, South America, and even Russia, not returning to the platform until 1913.*

---

* He was present in 1910 and led the prayer at the missionary meeting. His wife (Grubb married in 1906) helped at the Ladies Meeting. He died in 1940, aged 84. E. C. Millard worked independently in China and Armenia and died of a heart attack at Farnham, Surrey, early in 1900, aged 38. He was father of Frank Millard, for thirty-five years C.S.S.M. missioner in South Africa.

When Bowker died, Robert Wilson's appointment as chairman of the Convention had been unanimous. Talk of forming a "Council of Advice" went no further than increasing Trustees to five, including Hopkins and Wilson's son George, and naming Wilson Chairman of Trustees as well as of the Convention. Trustee duties remained confined to property,* but Wilson would call a committee of speakers and friends once during each Convention to advise on general matters.

Wilson made an excellent chairman, brief and punctual in the chair, and with a special Quaker gift of imparting an expectant reverence, thoroughly trusted in business, and possessing, as E. W. Moore said, "large and catholic sympathies." The growth of the Keswick Mission brought an increasing burden of correspondence, decisions, accounts, on an ageing man already much in demand as chairman of the local Conventions,** with no assistance except from the cumbrous informal committee which met once a year at Keswick. "The fact is," Fox warned Wilson in December 1895, "you have been bearing the heat and burden of the day thrice over and half a dozen men's work and worry—and in between public and private burdens, you have had a deep and exhausting heart-burden in our dear child Amy [Carmichael] and her vicissitudes and exile. . . . You must be more than careful this winter."

---

* Their legal title until 1901 was "Trustees of the Battersby Memorial Fund."
** These offshoots of Keswick were extending rapidly, e.g. (with dates of origin): Glasgow (1882), Belfast (1887), Dublin (1889), Birmingham (1890), Guildford (1890), Scottish National, Bridge of Allan (1892), Llandrindod Wells (1903), Killarney (1905), Portstewart (1914).

Some of the leaders grew restless at Wilson's benevolent dictatorship. A trivial incident brought matters to a head.

Late in 1895 a well-known lawyer, Reader Harris, who considered Keswick lukewarm and had founded the Pentecostal League of Prayer, alleged publicly that the Keswick Mission Fund was £100 in debt. He refused to be fobbed off by a hasty letter to the papers from Webb-Peploe: he demanded figures. "Reader Harris seems determined to go on bothering about the Keswick a/cs.," Hopkins wrote from his Kensington vicarage to Wilson on January 29, 1896. "People have been speaking to me about them, and I am ashamed to say I know nothing really about them, except what the others know, and yet I am one of the Trustees. This I feel must be remedied." He pointed out that if anything happened to Wilson there was no one abreast of the exact position; accounts were not audited; the Mission Committee was not even properly constituted, being merely a large ad hoc gathering of speakers and Trustees. Between Conventions no one knew who were members: it was "a multitude, that has no *head*, no *body* and no *tail*!" Hopkins wanted to see "the whole matter on a real business footing."

Webb-Peploe wished to go further and reverted to the plan for a Keswick "Inner Council of Advice" which should be responsible, under Wilson, for all the arrangements of Keswick and, he hinted, have power to exclude those such as Grubb and E. W. Moore whom Peploe ranked heretics.

Wilson talked matters over with Stock at Broughton Grange in March. He was ready for a Mission Council but a little hurt at the suggestion of a body to run the Convention. John Harford, who favored it, warmly assured him, "*You* are of course *Head* of the *spiritual side*, as well as of the financial and business side." Wilson called a meeting for April 24, 1896, to be held in Fox's church room at Eaton Chapel.

Fox persuaded Harford not to press for an "Inner Council" but Harford found Webb-Peploe, who was not a Trustee, stiff and determined: "He did not feel he could go on as he was going on now any longer, and that either he must be trusted and consulted or else he must withdraw altogether and appear no more at Keswick." Fox and Harford "agreed that it would be disastrous to have a split," and that an Inner Council, with Peploe on it, under Wilson's chairmanship, was essential. They did not wish to press this at the forthcoming meeting but feared Peploe would, and that acrimony might develop.

Wilson fell ill in April and his son George represented him at the meeting on April 24th. Fox, as host, took the chair and about twenty, including several ladies, were present.

The first that Wilson heard was a telegram at 4:30 p.m. from Miss Eva Bradshaw to Broughton Grange: "Prayer answered for Committee meeting. Spirit present." Next day came a penciled letter from George: "The meeting this afternoon was a very harmonious one—resulting in the formation of a Mission Committee subject to the sanction of the Trustees. . . . Nothing was said about the constituency of the Keswick Convention managt. except what I said in emphasizing your letter. Mr. Peploe raised no question on this head at all."

A letter from Fox as chairman told how "Peploe's opening prayer was excellent, full of tenderness and generous appreciation of you and adding, we want no more than that things may remain as they are under you if only you might be fully restored and preserved—he seemed thoroughly soft-

ened and feared his suggestions had been misunderstood. . . ."
The letter ended with a typical Fox double, of joke and encouragement: "The Chairman was the weakest part of the
meeting, *but we knew he meant well tho' he was rather forlorn
and out of his element!* We prayed like a hailstorm for you.
May God just heal you outright and keep you as our head-
piece for many years—we don't want a better and shouldn't
find one if we did."

The Keswick Convention Mission Council was set up,
with Chairman, Secretary, Treasurer; the Trustees ex-officio
and twenty-one elected members, retiring in rotation but
eligible for re-election. Executive and Ladies' subcommittees were appointed and Gen. Hatt-Noble elected Chairman (they had to clear another Webb-Peploe hurdle there;
he thought it should be always an Anglican clergyman).

The Mission had thus given Keswick its first proper organization although it was not until the winter of 1900-01,
when Wilson's health broke completely, that the management of the Convention itself was placed on a firm footing
by making the Trustees the executive head, with Hopkins
their Chairman.

# Thirteen

## Men of the Motto

To a Convention in the early 1890s came a Nonconformist minister on his first visit, to cover it for the *British Weekly*. He seems to have been in sympathy from the start, whereas the *British Weekly* man in 1889 had written scathingly—but before the despatch appeared the Convention had "put me right-about-face . . . a turning point in my life and ministry," and his second article, composed alone on the slopes of Skiddaw, had been different.

The correspondent of the nineties arrived by one of the special direct expresses from London. In the railway age before motors, the London and North-Western ran three or four specials one after another at the start of the Convention, and a shuttle service from Penrith for passengers from other parts—all converging on the twisting little branch to Keswick, where could be seen (in the words of another visitor) "the crowd on the platform, the piles of bags, hold-alls and portmanteaus, the anxiety of those who had lost their luggage, the rapturous greetings of friends. . . ."[*]

---

[*] H. B. Macartney in 1893. If there was anxiety, presumably this was the arrival, before the Convention!

The Convention had already taken on its familiar aspect—enterprising religious booksellers staffed temporary stalls on the street outside the Tent, and mission societies for home or abroad each had their site, generally then a gypsy-like caravan plastered with slogans and information. The Convention now ran from Monday night to Saturday morning, but the weekends virtually were part. On the Sundays the various churches opened pulpits to Keswick speakers of their denominations, and the Vicar of St. John's, J. N. Hoare, also held a succession of early Holy Communion services. Hoare, Harford-Battersby's immediate successor, continued the tradition of offering St. John's for the United Communion (using the Anglican liturgy) on Thursday morning. He did not himself attend Convention meetings but established a lasting precedent of hospitality irrespective of personal attitude; most subsequent Vicars were not in sympathy, except for Herbert Gresford-Jones (1904–06), an occasional Keswick speaker, later Bishop of Warrington.

"A printed program supplies a list of the meetings officially arranged," *British Weekly* readers were told, "which includes early morning prayer meetings, Bible readings, meetings for those attending the Convention the first time, special meetings for ministers, for ladies, for young men and for children. . . . With short intervals for refreshments meetings succeeded one another all through the day, and the astonishing fact remains that there seemed no disposition to wander away, nor the slightest indication of weariness." About this spiritual gormandizing (the thought of which may dizzy a less patient generation) the correspondent had one regret. "My only regret as a Nonconformist is that a movement like this, so entirely scriptural and beneficial, is falling so largely into the hands of the Church of England, simply because the leaders of Nonconformity are holding aloof from it. . . . Keswick Convention is a great institution, and it will be a thousand pities if our Nonconformist leaders withhold from it their sympathy and support."

Nevertheless in these years non-Anglicans were emerging at last to right the balance and give point to the motto *All one in Christ Jesus.* Except for the cheerful, lovable middle-aged Lancashire Methodist John Brash, who had been preaching and living "Scriptural holiness" for years before the Oxford Conference but was not invited to the Keswick platform until the nineties—perhaps because he had never been to college—most of them were younger men.

Of the three who were important to the Keswick story the most famous was F. B. Meyer.

Frederick Brotherton Meyer, future President of the Free Church Federal Council and of the Baptist Union, prolific and popular writer, social reformer, pastor in York, Leicester and London, moved by slow stages towards an honored and regular place at Keswick.

In his first independent charge at York, Meyer "didn't know anything about conversion, or about the gathering of sinners around Christ"—until the then unknown Moody and Sankey came to his church in the summer of 1873 within a few days of the inauspicious start of the campaign that was to sweep England. Meyer's invitation had been a little grudging; revival broke out in spite of him, and through Moody "I learned how to point men to God."

Next year he attended the Oxford Conference. His spiritual life, beneath a ministry markedly successful outwardly, remained "spasmodic and fitful, now flaming up with enthusiasm, and then pacing wearily over leagues of grey ashes and cold cinders"—until C. T. Studd and Stanley Smith of the Cambridge Seven visited Leicester in November 1884 when Meyer was thirty-seven. "I saw that these young men had something which I had not, but which was to them a constant source of rest and joy." At seven in the morning following their meeting, he paid a visit to their lodgings and found they had already been long at their Bibles. Meyer asked "How can I be like you?" Charley Studd inquired if Meyer had ever "given yourself to Christ, for Christ to fill you?" "Yes, in a general sort of way, but I don't know that I have done it particularly." The talk that the three had then, Meyer called "one of the formative influences of my life."

Keswick sought never to invite a new speaker unless he had proved himself at local conventions and was known too, by character and outlook, to have experience of what he preached. Meyer had passed these tests when invited in 1887. He was not asked, however—again according to custom— to deliver an address. This was as well, for he retained a strong consciousness of inward poverty.

One evening after the close of the official meeting a number remained for prayer in the Tent and, because Grubb led them, grew vociferous. Meyer crept "under the tent" and walked into the night—up Manor Brow and towards the high ground—feeling "the time had come when I must get everything or have a broken heart. . . . Stars were shining, and now and again a cloud drifted across and the lake was there below me, shimmering, and the moon was breaking on the scene and there was the lovely breath of wind. I walked to and fro, and said to God: 'I must have the best, I cannot go on living like this.'" He seemed to hear God's voice to his soul, "Breathe in the air, breathe it in; and as you breathe it in your lungs, let there be an intake from God." There was not: a sin or habit, "one tough bit," remained too sweet or strong. Then Meyer remembered words of C. T. Studd in their talk three years earlier, and spoke again to his Lord: "I am not willing, but I am willing to be made willing." In the quiet of the hillside he opened his whole being.

He felt no surge of feeling, so that George Grubb later that night doubted the validity of the experience. Meyer disagreed: "Though I do not feel it, I reckon God is faithful," and his ministry from thenceforth showed him right.

Meyer's influence on Keswick, at home and during overseas deputations, was as strong as its influence on him; in the course of time he brought it the prestige that grew around his name in nation and Nonconformity. His preaching had a sympathetic simplicity which balanced the more theological disquisitions of his colleagues, and though in later years its quality was affected by his restlessness and constant travels (it was said the devil came to him in the guise of a railway train), and Keswick did not always have his best, he delivered some of the greatest addresses ever heard there.*

Meyer was a stout controversialist when in early middle age, and the religious press once accused him of breaking an unwritten rule of Keswick by distributing Baptist tracts in the Tent and urging rebaptism on Anglicans; it is believed that he rebaptized George Grubb, but the evidence is not firm. The phase passed. By the time Meyer reached sixty he was described as "buoyant as of old, but more mellow: his

---

* It is said that in the early 1900s he spoke on "Honesty and Restitution" with such effect that the town Post Office ran out of postal orders, and that this was the reason for the opening of an annual sub-office in Convention Lodge!

journeys to East and West seemed to have effaced the last trace of controversy." It might only be detected—apart from his willingness to drive into the thick of national battles, for social justice or moral order—in an unfortunate tendency to speak and write of "Keswick Teaching," the "Keswick Brotherhood," in that very way Webb-Peploe had so abhorred.

His personality had a winsomeness that made him one of the best loved of all the second generation of Keswick, and in old age, with his finely chiseled features, white hair and benign smile, it could be said of him that "Dr. Meyer was a saint and looked like one."

George Hogarth Carnaby Macgregor (the magnificent names being no indication of birth in a humble manse) was a tall, wiry young Highlander with coal-black hair and the Celt's blend of poetry and mysticism, energy and dash.

He was "a man intensely alive," wrote his cousin. "He had great powers of enjoyment, and threw himself heart and soul into everything." Almost tireless, mentally and physically, he thought nothing of a sixty- or eighty-mile ride on one of the new safety bicycles one day and a full program in his parish the next. He had great powers of concentration, could absorb rapidly a mass of ideas and information; his acumen and knowledge were fine tributes to Edinburgh University and New College where he trained for the ministry of the Free Church of Scotland. He also read novels—often at a sitting—at a time when godly folk were inclined to rate a novel as of the devil, by definition. He read his

Bible in the Hebrew and Greek texts and wrote all his sermons in shorthand.

George Macgregor was called to a city charge at Aberdeen a few weeks before his twenty-fourth birthday in 1888 and showed at once his desire: "May I win souls and build them up, that Thy Kingdom may be advanced."

He had two weak spots: a temper which, normally sweet, could produce paroxysms of rage; and worry. He knew he was "not what I ought to be." He went to the Keswick of 1889, at the close of his first year at Aberdeen, with motives blended of intellectual curiosity on the subject of sanctification, and a genuine anxiety for increased spiritual power. "I had not been in the place many minutes," he related four years later, "before I found the treatment was practical and new. Then I felt very angry, as a Scotsman, at being told anything new in theology by an Englishman." By their addresses Moule, Hopkins and Meyer each had a part in turning him inside out. To his sister he wrote: "I have been searched through and through, and bared and exposed and scorched by God's searching Spirit. And then I have learned the unsearchableness of Christ. How Christ is magnified here you can scarcely have any idea."

A Scottish friend happened to meet him at Strathpeffer immediately afterwards. "He was in the fullness of his new joy, soft from the making. He had gone to Keswick in critical mood. He left it disarmed. He was gripped, humbled, emptied and filled, and now he was as if heavenly wine were rushing in his veins."

Macgregor first spoke at the Convention of 1892 although only twenty-eight. His incisive speech (in a rich Highland accent), wide grasp of contemporary thought, unswerving loyalty to Christ and an almost boyish zest to impart *So Great Salvation* (the title of the short book he wrote in 1892), made him appreciated year after year, especially by young men from universities. Moody tried to persuade him to leave Britain for the Bible Institute and church at Chicago.

Macgregor at college had passed through a period of "scepticism and doubt. . . . I lost all faith in the Bible as inspired." Like many of his age he had been brought up to a mechanical view of inspiration, and it collapsed in the wave of revolutionary thought which had swept into theological colleges during the eighties, bred of the extremes of an over-confident higher criticism, of Darwin, and the rationalism that was fast gaining ground beyond the intellectual circles where it had flourished for several decades. From this phase of doubt Macgregor emerged with a stronger faith in the authority of the Bible as God's Word without losing sympathy for such as his friend the persecuted Robertson Smith who, he saw, "although a rigorous and scientific critic of the Bible, was a reverent and believing critic."

In the battles around inspiration and authority, which were to wreak such harm in Great Britain and America, George Macgregor might have done more than any other wholehearted evangelical leader to hold the churches to a true course, for he would have been at the height of his powers from about 1910 until 1930. He long had a premonition of early death. His elder brother and sister both died suddenly. In Scotland and at his later charge in London, in missions and convention journeys at home and overseas, he "preach'd as never sure to preach again, And as a dying man to dying men."

In the week following a crowded Easter he was struck

down by meningitis and died on May 3, 1900, at the age of thirty-five.

---

Charles Inwood was the son of a village tailor in Bedfordshire, a Methodist local preacher, and at eighteen in 1869 he accepted an unlikely call to help the Methodists of a remote part of Southern Ireland. Without benefit of college education he was ordained to the ministry of the Methodist Church of Ireland six years later.

He married an Irish girl. Twice in their first year she left him. Her strange and restless temperament produced a home background (to remain with him to the close of his life) which threatened to throttle his usefulness. In the words of one of his family:* "Victory had to be found, if his ministry were to be powerful in blessing and fruitfulness. He earnestly sought the Lord for it, and the Lord's answer was that fullness of the Holy Spirit which brought steadfast serenity to his inner life and gracious power to his ministry." Perhaps because he had little formal education the spiritual struggles of this Bedfordshire tailor's son had a titanic quality akin to those of Bunyan the Bedfordshire tinker, which made him the man he became.

A growing reputation as evangelist and convention speaker in Ireland led to the Keswick platform in 1892 when he was already forty-one, and the tone of his first address was unexpected and characteristic: he attacked "counterfeit consecration." He was fearless. He had power to grip his

---

* In a letter to the author.

hearers and force them to face personal attitudes and habits —which contemporary humbug tolerated—and then to display the power of the Holy Spirit, his constant theme. His approach was that of a surgeon, not of a ranter, though it had emotional force. It cut so close to the nerve that on the Tuesday of Keswick 1894, when Inwood rebuked "unclean chambers of imagery" in the minds of Christians, censured "the tendency to bow before the latest fashion in science and theology," and attacked the "filthy habit of smoking" (thousands of worthy evangelical males of the period puffed at pipes nearly as large as their walrus mustaches) he aroused widespread resentment, especially among the smokers. "All I knew," Inwood recounted eleven years later, "was, I had got my message from God, and I kept obeying Him in the delivery of it." He had to hide himself "quietly before God" all Wednesday, until at the Bible Reading on Thursday morning "God gave us a Pentecost." Scores of men abandoned smoking. Some presented pipes to speakers as "mementoes of the victories of God's grace," others went and threw theirs into the lake, and one batch collected all their pipes—including some costly and elaborate—made a fire, and solemnly reduced them to ashes.

The severity of Inwood's speaking had a balance of "affectionate pleading. Look how frequently," writes one close to him, "he interspersed the word 'Beloved' in his addresses. That was no pious ejaculation but sprang from real tenderness"; he was not severe off the platform, though he never secured a wide circle of friends nor veered towards the jocular. A man who publicly sets a lofty standard of holiness, especially if he etches in the outline by detailed assessment of current social customs, may sometimes be privately hard and unlovely, forgetful that true holiness concerns attitudes as well as habits. Not Inwood. Those who knew him best loved him most. He really did maintain, with barely a stumble, kindliness, serenity and chivalry in a continuously exasperating predicament which he never disclosed.

Inwood formed, with Macgregor and Hubert Brooke, the Keswick deputation to Canada in 1893. Four years later he offered to the Keswick Mission Council "my entire time and life to this work," having grown increasingly certain that he had received a call as clear as any to a missionary, although it might ruin his future with the Methodist Church of Ireland. He went to North America, Sweden and Germany for Keswick in 1897, and, with his wife, to China in 1898, and thus shouldered George Grubb's mantle, though no two men could have been more dissimilar.

Before, during, and after the First World War Charles Inwood moved across the continents. He developed a remarkable gift for speaking through interpretation. National Christians in missionary lands of an imperial age were drawn by his affectionate simplicity and approachability. A young missionary was allotted an evangelist who was anti-British. When the national discovered the Englishman to be Inwood's son-in-law his manner changed: "He gave me his confidence and I enjoyed some unforgettable years of service with him." "The truths for which Keswick stands," Inwood wrote in a letter of 1912, "become more dear to my soul every year, and I find ever increasing joy and blessing in making them known."

As if to symbolize that Keswick was now fully interdenominational and international, the Convention of 1895 was outstandingly that of Andrew Murray. This was the only appearance at Keswick as a speaker of the great Scottish-Boer prophet of the Dutch Reformed Church, by then a "dear old man . . . so thin and worn-looking."

One woman wrote to her friends: "I cannot describe to you the deep, solemn, heart-searching teaching of Mr. Murray's evening addresses, nor the power and authority with which they were delivered." Murray tended to draw his hearers towards a somewhat rarified faith, as if Christlikeness were possible only by withdrawal from large areas of human activity; but in the context of the Convention—where his thought-forms were fully understood and other speakers provided, unconsciously, an equilibrium—Murray deepened devotion and understanding to an extraordinary degree, and "opened up a vista of infinite and inexhaustible capacity." Through the disruptive years of the South African war (in which Murray's loyalty lay with the Boers) and for as long as memory lasted, men and women looked back in awe and gratitude to his final address on the Friday night: "That God may be all in all."

At the prayer meeting on the following morning Murray rose to leave the moment it closed, in order to catch his train to sail for America. The whole audience rose spontaneously, sang *God be with you till we meet again,* and then "stood in respectful silence until he had passed out of the Tent."*

---

* W. B. Sloan in *These Sixty Years* (p. 43) makes no mention of the singing and says Murray left early. He was writing after forty years. Mrs. Albert Head described the scene in a letter after only six days, August 1, 1895 (*The Life of Mrs. Albert Head*, p. 174).

# Fourteen

---

# Trans-Atlantic Traffic

W ebb-Peploe, that self-constituted censor, complained to Wilson in 1895 that he and Moule would lose influence "with our fellow Churchmen, if the rising teachers of the K[eswick] P[latform] are not somewhat more drawn from the ranks of the Church. . . . I am constantly hearing now from many quarters that the whole movement is leaving the Church of England rapidly and that the new speakers are almost entirely Dissenters." Fortunately he received short shrift. General Hatt-Noble, as devoted an Anglican, expressed the more general view: "If the Keswick Convention departs from the pan-denominational lines I fear I should have to leave it. We want the union of all who love the Lord Jesus in sincerity, be they Methodists, Presbyterians, Friends, Baptists, etc., to be cemented, not narrowed or contracted."

General Noble put his finger on another problem. "I am pained to see that Keswick is becoming overgrown and a Convention for the rich alone. . . . I think our poor saints as worthy of consideration as the rich ones."

Certainly in those days there were Convention crawlers who (as Murray remarked) "come year to year to be edified and pleased, worshiping the Lord at Keswick, while heart and life are not given up to His service." "We are five again in the same dear little house," runs the diary of Miss Florence Sitwell, daughter of a deceased Yorkshire baronet and landowner. "Mother has brought George the footman (we hope it may do him good; he may be drawn in without knowing), but no maid. We were out this morning at seven for prayer, and then a meeting in the tent. . . . Mr. Inwood spoke exceedingly well on the Lowering of Moral Tone by Fiction of the present day, and the Spiritual witnessing of God that should take its place. A thunderstorm later . . ." "A wonderful, beautiful, helpful time at Keswick," she writes at the close. "Keswick seems to me, and I think to Mother, a little bit of Heaven."

Two or three houseparties for millworkers and an influx of shipbuilding operatives from Barrow on their half holiday were usual by the late nineties, but inequalities of wealth deferred a democratic complexion until times should change.*

Two expansions in this vigorous decade widened and strengthened Keswick's footing.

Robert Wilder of Pennsylvania had touched off, at Moody's first college conference in Massachusetts in 1886, the meteoric rise of the Student Volunteer Missionary Union. Over 6,000 Student Volunteers had signed a card indicating willingness to serve overseas if God should call, and 350 of

---

* In one sense time seems standing still. "We hope to be in our old lodgings at Keswick . . . but with the steadily rising prices of lodgings and everything else I fear we shall have to make change in our arrangements." A letter of General Hatt-Noble, June 5, 1896!

them were already on the field, when in July 1891 this twenty-eight year old American landed in England with an introduction to Eugene Stock.

Stock said the best avenue to Christian students in Britain lay through the imminent Keswick Convention and despatched Wilder to fill the last vacancy in the family houseparty of Mrs. MacInnes, wife of a Cumberland M.P. and mother of a Cambridge undergraduate. Wilder arrived at their country estate near Carlisle for the weekend preceding the Convention (and promptly asked for a stenographer and a typewriter). On the Sunday, the MacInneses happened to take Wilder to hear a Salvation Army officer. He preached about a "clean heart." Wilder went to see him later "and left more perplexed than when I entered, but I knew the man had something which was very real and very beautiful. I began to pray for purity of motive and purity of heart such as I never knew before." Before the houseparty moved to Keswick, Wilder had written some difficult letters to colleagues in America with whom he had quarreled, and had received the answer to his prayer, "Create in me a clean heart, O God, and renew a right spirit within me."

Had the American not heard the Salvation Army officer, his visit to Keswick would have come too soon. Had he begun to propagate his scheme for Volunteers before the end of the Convention, he would have spoken too soon.

One of the "large sprinkling of youths from the Scottish and English universities," Donald Fraser, a Glasgow divinity student bogged in philosophical doubt, had joined the small camp organized by the Y.M.C.A. because a five pound note had been given him for the purpose. The Convention meetings "irritated me beyond measure." He sat at the back of the choir (male students and young ladies at opposite sides of the platform) doodling caricatures of the speakers. Slowly he felt the grip "of the awful sin of unbelief and of the moral helplessness of one who fought alone." On the Thursday evening, in deep depression, so he told Hopkins years after, "Something you said about moral liberty—I mean, the unloosing of the bonds of sin—which comes with the presence of the Spirit, suddenly awoke me. I do not now remember the mental process by which I came to liberty. But the next thing I do remember is weeping like a fool in my own tent under an awful sense of my sin of unbelief, and dedicating myself to God, accepting the wonder of the Trinity, and receiving the blessed Guest Himself into my life. Two days after, Wilder spoke. . . ."

In 1927 Donald Fraser said: "Had Mr. Wilder spoken the year before or even some days before, the Student Movement might not have happened. But a band of students from the Scottish and English universities had been specially prepared by the Convention for the word he brought." That Saturday morning Wilder spoke last, after thirteen graphic talks by serving missionaries (including Charles Harford from the Niger), and the clock had ticked away two hours and forty minutes. Yet his brief tale of the Student Volunteers in America, followed by words shaped closely on Hudson Taylor's famous appeal to the Perth Conference of 1865, burned into the consciousness of every young man. Fraser stretched out a hand to the Scot beside him: "We must do something for the men in our Hall next winter."

On the lake that afternoon the two Scots planned for Scottish Volunteers, then called on Wilder and begged him to visit Glasgow. "I had always felt a drawing to be a missionary, but abandoned the intention during my doubting days. Wilder's speech," Fraser wrote after years of distinguished service in Nyasaland and for the whole missionary cause,* "kindled a fire which has grown only intenser with the years."

Fraser raised Student Volunteers in Scotland. Undergraduates invited Wilder to Cambridge. By the following Easter an S.V.M.U. of Great Britain had been inaugurated, and in 1893 the Student Volunteers held their first Camp, of about one hundred and forty men, at Keswick immediately before the Convention.

The choice of time and place brought the benefit of experienced missionaries who specially reached Keswick early, while all campers but a handful stayed on under canvas for the Convention.

Convention spirit pervaded Camp. At the first meeting campers were urged to pick on "one uncomely characteristic" in their personalities and to claim Christ's total victory over it. Temple Gairdner from Oxford, not yet a Volunteer, chose "cowardice, physical and moral." On the third day he and J. H. Oldham went out beside Derwent Water for prayer and "did not rise till we had claimed light through Christ and received it." Gairdner felt he "would not mind being beaten for Christ," and believed he was "right with God." On the Saturday afternoon when Keswick was filling with Convention attenders, some of the campers went on the lake for a meeting, "the sun shining overhead, the water as calm as

---

* Dr. Donald Fraser (1870–1933) is one of the comparatively few missionaries who were noticed in the *Dictionary of National Biography*. The new (2004) *Oxford Dictionary of National Biography* which replaces DNB includes many, including Hudson Taylor and CT Studd.

glass, the birds singing in the trees," Fraser recalls. The impressively rugged Robert Stewart from Fukien stood in the stern of a boat giving an informal talk. His words belied the placid setting: "Christ suffered in agony," he cried, "so must we! Christ died, so perhaps may we. Our lives *must* be hard, cruel, wearisome, unknown. So was His. . . . Gentlemen, the measure of your success will be the measure of your *agonia*!"

This last phrase rang in Gairdner's mind through the Convention until one afternoon, alone, he crept into St. John's Church to face his future. It narrowed to the question: "Canst thou drink of the cup that I drink of, and be baptized with the baptism wherewith I was baptized?" Reverently and humbly Gairdner rose, and as if he could see Christ before whom he stood, answered: "I can."

Gairdner died in Cairo in 1928 in his mid-fifties, not violently but from the rigors of valiant service. For Stewart of China his own words were prophetic: two years later almost to the day, he called his fellow missionaries in Fukien to a "little Keswick" coinciding with the Convention in England. They ended with Holy Communion and early the following morning Stewart, his wife, two of his children and six women colleagues were murdered by Chinese in cold blood.

Another undergraduate, Douglas Thornton of Cambridge, had been less impressed by the Volunteer conference, though it deepened determination to serve abroad; but at the Convention, in the "crowded and stifling" Drill Hall, where overflow meetings took place, "H. B. Macartney rose up full of the Holy Ghost. He electrified everyone in a word, so it seemed to me, by asking them to say together, 'I believe in the Holy Ghost.' We all did . . . I had confessed my faith in Him," Thornton writes, "and He came in all his fullness into my soul. Immediately I seemed to see Jesus. . . ." The moment Macartney finished, Thornton jumped out of the nearest window and dashed down to the Market Place, begging to be allowed to testify at the Open Air.

Thornton, the vehement puritan from Cambridge, Gairdner, vigorous and artistic from Oxford, and the genial Highlander, Fraser from Glasgow, swept the Student Volunteers forward. Keswick had cradled all three, and Fraser, some twenty years on, wrote that "the Convention created in our colleges the atmosphere which made the Student Movement possible." The early milestones were each passed at Keswick, at Convention or Student Conference: 1893, the formation of the Inter-Universities Christian Union (afterwards British College Christian Union);* 1894, the adoption of the American Volunteers watchword, "The Evangelization of the World in This Generation," when Robert Speer came from the United States; 1895, with the Americans John R. Mott and Luther Wishard present, the preliminary decision to form a World's Student Christian Federation. The early Student Movement reached a climax at its Liverpool Conference over the new year, 1896.

The Volunteers moved from Keswick to Swanwick in 1898, not for cleavage of principle or practice but to exchange a camp for a conference house and to avoid appearing a subsidiary of the Convention. Nevertheless the trends which eventually deflected the Student Movement's course emerged after the change and the departure of the early leaders overseas.

---

* The two formally federated in 1898 and in 1905 took the name of Student Christian Movement of Great Britain and Ireland.

Wilder, Speer, Mott, Wishard. The Student Volunteers not only clinched Keswick and universities; they thickened Keswick's transatlantic traffic.

Keswick's springs had been in America. Though Pearsall Smith never saw Derwent Water, an American or two would be in every Convention audience and occasionally on his or her feet: for instance, Amanda Smith the negress, who spoke at the Ladies' Meeting in the eighties.

Closer intercourse followed D. L. Moody's brief visit in 1892. As far back as 1880 Moody had summoned "hungry Christians" to the first Northfield Conference at his Massachusetts hometown "for solemn self-consecration, for pleading God's promises, and waiting upon Him for a fresh anointment of power from on high." The Northfield gatherings were an informal, rather haphazard blend of Mildmay and the "Christian Convention" which ended each Moody and Sankey campaign and a devotional convocation. When he discovered Keswick, its progressive teaching, concentration on the spiritual need of the individual Christian, and its context of unity and service, Moody, who always grasped for Northfield and America any good thing to strengthen the churches, began to organize an import.

Hubert Brooke, Macgregor and Inwood, on their way to Canadian deputation in April of 1893, were brought to Northfield for two days to address Moody's schools, and subsequently spent a week in Chicago around Moody's Bible Institute. For the Northfield Conference that summer Moody sent for his old friend F. B. Meyer "and asked me to come over and help him; and there in that sweet New England village I unfolded the blessed message of deliverance from the power of known sin." Meyer, a curiously childlike egotist, seems to have imagined he was creating the very first Conference. His "new teaching," as he insisted on calling it, caused Moody's "Old Guard," including R. A. Torrey, the Superintendent of the Bible Institute at Chicago, and C. I. Scofield, the Northfield pastor, future editor of the Scofield Reference Bible, to lodge heavy protests. Moody had to run around keeping the peace.

Meyer returned four years in succession, Torrey and Scofield having at length understood his drift. Moody pushed Meyer's books and early in 1897, as part of a drive to deepen the life of the churches, had him over for a whirlwind campaign in the cities of the Atlantic Coast. The *Sunday School Times* of Philadelphia understood that "Mr. Moody has expressed the desire to make Northfield the American Keswick." The Conference, however, still had a less-pointed purpose and although, after Moody's death in 1899, a Keswick speaker would still be a feature of every summer conference, neither Northfield nor other American centers developed a close counterpart.

In 1895 Andrew Murray and Webb-Peploe went straight from Keswick to Northfield and beyond. (Fox wrote to Wilson that December: "Peploe gave a graphic account of his travels with limelight pictures the other night for *three* mortal hours on end without a break, i.e., from 8 o'clock to 11 o'clock at night. Think of it! It's the best thing I've heard him do.") At Northfield the world's chief exponent of the missionary claim, the distinguished American pastor who on Spurgeon's death had filled his pulpit, eminent member of the Northfield platform, the fifty-eight-year-old Dr. Arthur T. Pierson, heard Murray and Peploe tell of "the power of God as to character," and awoke to the humiliation that his own undoubted consecration and honored service had left pride, impatience and self-will. When the Keswick speakers asked those to stand who needed to claim God's power, he stood, in costly confession.

Pierson spoke at Keswick in 1897, 1898, and six Conventions after. "His voice had tones like a bell. His eye had the quality of needles." He was also a problem to his hostess for he had dieting fads and the appetite of an elderly mouse.

In 1904 R. A. Torrey, during a pause in the Torrey-Alexander missions, traveled to Keswick as a listener. At the railway station the Trustees told him Webb-Peploe had been called away by family illness and would Dr. Torrey please deliver the Bible Readings? Torrey's great series on "The Holy Spirit," at such short notice, and Pierson's general addresses dovetailed the United States and the Platform. Should a suitable American be in England, Keswick leaped at the opportunity—but not, at that time, to the point of paying for a special journey.

American voices, American insights, American warmth and friendliness and grasp of the Bible were welcome ingredients, appreciated the more every decade. With much that enhanced Keswick's value, Pierson and Torrey introduced one less valuable constituent. A journalist said Dr. Pierson's brain "seemed to be a set of pigeonholes, alphabetically arranged"; Torrey had trained his massive intellect to present doctrines in pithy, ordered snippets for easy digestion by his Bible Institute students. The two had been impressed by Keswick's consecutive unfolding of the theme of sanctification, each day's addresses building on the previous, and they promptly pressed this into a close-knit system. Pierson even laid down a "Keswick Plan . . . definite, complete and progressive," having "a definite Beginning, Course and Culmination," Six Successive Steps "to and in the blessed life." Somewhat oddly, "Aim a deadly blow at self (be dead to Ambition, Avarice, Appetite and the amusing and alluring Pleasures of the World)" was the second step in Pierson's peculiar Plan, placed right back two steps before "the Infilling of the Spirit"; thereby—though nobody seems to have noticed —sabotaging the entire ethos of "the blessed life."

Such codifying encouraged lesser minds to narrow, for a period, Keswick's exposition. It could not contract the truth.

# Fifteen

## Welsh Fire

The turn of the century thinned the ranks. Macgregor's sudden death at Easter 1900, the retirement of Wilson, the death of Fox.

Robert Wilson, his heavy shoulders more bowed each year, shaggy head whiter, eyes retaining their gentle twinkle, developed a throat affliction that stifled speech. He took the chair last in 1900. The reins slipped his aged fingers; the Trustees assumed full executive control with Evan Hopkins as Chairman. Wilson's health confined him to Broughton Grange, quietly and painlessly, for five years of a true Quaker eventide until he died, without fuss, at his dining room table, lunching alone on a June day of 1905 in sight of the hills.

Charles Fox's end—just as fine a Christian evidence—contrasted tragically with Wilson's. Fox had struggled through the Convention of '99 to learn in September that he had cancer of the face. Despite an operation, the weary months before his death in December 1900 brought agony which the devotion of doctors and of his wife could do little to alleviate. Faith expressed itself in verse, especially in his poem *The Marred Face*, where he drew comfort from Isaiah's words on the Suffering Servant, and in letters scrawled in pauses from pain: "How strange, and yet how dear, suffering with Christ! It is dying daily, but with Him. He knows, He loves, He suffers."

The Convention grew.

For 1894 an extra tent had been rented, and the following years a fine pavilion by the riverside, until in 1900 the trustees bought and leveled the Skiddaw Street plot—for which a Miss DuPre of Kingston-on-Thames gave a new tent, used in 1901, "exactly like the first one in all dimensions." Each tent was equal, and "to make this more clear the names of the speakers at all the main meetings in both Tents are to be printed on the notice boards," breaking custom and tempting swarms around popular speakers. The running of the simultaneous series slightly weakened impact, but the size of any tent had to be dictated by the strength of voices (unaided by amplifiers of the future), and the numbers of those who wished to listen rose yearly. Each tent could hold a total of three thousand and it was estimated, probably with slight exaggeration, that "not less than six thousand persons are present for the whole or part," with day visitors inflating this figure.

Vigor kept pace with growth.

A "Keswick Circle of Prayer" was inaugurated in 1902, informally without subscription or card, and in 1903 a Speakers' Prayer Conference took place, the speakers arriving in time to spend Saturday at St. John's Vicarage where Barclay Buxton was temporaily residing; a proper Prayer Conference had to wait until Evan Hopkins, turning seventy, resigned his Kensington living to devote himself to conventions and bought a spacious house in Surrey where speakers mustered for two June days from 1907. *Hymns of Consecration and Faith* was revised in 1903, and a second revision began shortly before the First World War; and in 1903— proof of the Christian public's appetite— the Trustees were invited to extend future Conventions to two weeks, "the first to be taken up with Bible study." Wisely they declined. The Convention had already virtually stretched itself to nine days, from Saturday evening's preliminary meeting to the church services on the second Sunday.

For all its vigor, Keswick could not remain untouched by contemporary pressures. Shifting social standards, bitter political and sectarian controversies, daring theological theories which roared into accepted attitudes with the noise and speed of the new horseless carriages now churning up dusty, rolling English roads, made the early years of Edward VII— from a longer perspective apparently so placid—a time of unsettlement and change.

Some wished Keswick to march onward and upward with liberal Protestantism towards the millennium around the corner, and were repelled because the doctrines of the Atonement and the Second Coming were not dismissed. Others wished Keswick to rebut and condemn.

Hopkins drew up in 1902 a "sketch of the usual line of teaching" for the new speakers. Was this a tacit admission that new speakers lacked depth? After the 1904 Convention an attender wrote: "In days when painful controversies distract the Church of Christ, the testimony of Keswick to the unity of the Spirit in the bond of peace grows ever clearer and more precious." Would peace be achieved only by withdrawal into contemplation? A generation earlier Keswick had been forward, pioneering, its principles attacked as dangerously new; now, inevitably, it seemed conservative, its principles disdained as old-fashioned; would it turn negative, defensive? The makers of Keswick had been predominantly younger men; their survivors were nearing or over seventy, and if no elderly clergymen were seen flanking a speaker with uplifted ear-trumpets reminiscent "of elephants raising their trunks to Buddha" (as once at Mildmay), and if men for the twentieth century already were prominent (such as dapper little Stuart Holden, the analytical, strong-voiced Campbell Morgan, and the energetic Bishop Taylor Smith on brief leaves from his duties as Chaplain-General), did the Convention rely upon the slackening momentum of the founders?

Were the truths taught at Keswick eternal or Victorian? The answer came strangely.

———  ———  ———

Jessie Penn-Lewis, then about forty, was one of those women like Florence Nightingale who were of such fragility that they expected to die any moment yet survived prodigious labors to great age. Welsh, married to an Englishman, the City Accountant of Leicester, she had formerly been a parishioner of Evan Hopkins and was embarked on a worldwide if rather one-tracked convention ministry. At the Convention of 1902, where she gave addresses at the Ladies' Meetings, she was approached by two Welsh ministers who told her that for six years they had prayed for a Keswick in Wales.

Next month she discussed the idea with the aged Dean of St. Davids, the great David Howell, and neither his death nor a dash to India by Mrs. Penn-Lewis prevented the first Convention at Llandrindod Wells, in the center of Wales, opening a week after Keswick 1903, with Hopkins, Meyer, Stuart Holden and Mrs. Penn-Lewis on the platform and Albert Head, London banker and Keswick Trustee, in the chair.

Among the hundreds present were six young ministers from North Wales, close friends, who had long sought confusedly for spiritual power. "That Convention was an utterly new and strange experience," one of the six, R. B. Jones, records. "Those young men returned to their pulpits altogether changed." During the following months several of the six, continues Jones, "without the least collusion found themselves preaching from Isaiah's vision of the Holy, Holy, Holy God, and His call to solemn service. The light, as they preached, was intense and the conviction deep. Everywhere was heard the echo of Isaiah's cry, 'Woe is me, for I am undone.'" The six met monthly, and at the second Llandrindod Wells Convention they prayed at midnight, "consecrated themselves afresh and definitely asked the Lord to raise up someone to usher in the Revival." Flames were flickering elsewhere: youths after long days in mine or quarry were stealing quietly to mountainsides for prayer; local conventions were springing up in South and Central Wales, burdened with the urge for holiness. In September 1904, young Evan Roberts, former coal miner now studying for the ministry—lean, genial, awkward in speech and manner—underwent the cataclysmic experience that swiftly, unexpectedly, brought him to the leadership of a movement which soon blazed across Wales.

Although Nonconformists were affected the most, Anglicans too felt the flames. "The churches are united in a solid phalanx," a newspaper reported of one town. "The prayer meetings are so crowded that the places of worship are inadequate to contain them. Some last eight hours. . . ." The press soon reported the extraordinary happenings in Wales because a new spirit began to pervade industry. "I was then a lad who had just started work in the coal mines," recalls the former Labour cabinet minister, James Griffiths. "The Revival invaded the pit: the morning spell became a prayer meeting." The South Wales papers gave pages and the London *Daily News* touchingly described pit ponies bewildered because haulers, "as a class proverbial for their profanity and cruelty," were no longer accompanying their orders with oaths and blows.

The Welsh Revival wherever it swept, or broke out in spontaneous spiritual combustion, soon showed certain characteristics. R. B. Jones is supported by other evidence in his memory that "the outstanding feature of those days [was] the universal, inescapable sense of the presence of God, felt in the Revival gatherings, felt also in the homes, on the streets, in the mines and factories, in the schools, even in the theaters and drinking saloons." Wales rediscovered worship, and expressed it, as ever, in song.

Undoubtedly there were excesses and paroxysms, as in the days of Whitefield's and Wesley's vast outdoor preachings when tears furrowed the coal grime on miners' faces; Reader Harris noted how as "Confession follows confession, the congregation takes up a hymn, and the great crowd sways and seethes. Wedged between uproar and hubbub, Evan Roberts makes an occasional brief appeal." Yet the silences were as remarkable as the singing and ejaculations; often a crowd would prolong worship without human leadership. And "the moral results," assessed the *Daily News*, "are making themselves seen and felt everywhere," not least by sharp falls in drunkenness and petty crime.

Revival began in each locality with loyal Christians discovering the feebleness, impurity and selfishness of their personal faith. A cleansed, revived church then found itself, almost unaware, a magnet for the lapsed, the impenitent and the faithless. It was this collective character of the Revival which impressed Evan Hopkins. "We have been accustomed," he wrote in January 1905, "to the Holy Spirit's working through the missioner or evangelist directly upon the unconverted. But what we are witnessing today is the same Divine power working through the Church in its corporate capacity on those who are unsaved."

———

Three hundred Welshmen came to the Keswick of 1905. The crowds there were larger than any, for in England Torrey and Alexander had brought hundreds into the churches or to new conceptions of service. A strong spirit of expectancy was heightened by a preliminary meeting on the Saturday morning, when R. B. Jones from Porth asked why the Revival had not spread more obviously beyond Wales: "Cannot this Convention set England on fire?"

Handley Moule, now Bishop of Durham, who had urged his clergy to welcome the Revival, was absent—ill—but A. T. Pierson from America and Charles Inwood had each spent several weeks in South Wales, and their addresses at the official opening on the Monday night—Pierson in the Skiddaw Street Tent, Inwood in Eskin Street—centered on it.

Inwood always spoke best when his emotions were charged: "I can never again be content with the ideals that in some measure satisfied me up to the time that I went to the Welsh Revival," he said, and urged that "God wants to use this single Convention as the instrument through which He shall let loose on England as mighty and sweeping a movement as He has sent down upon Wales. . . . I believe that God wants us to have an atmosphere in these meetings so tremulous with the Holy Spirit that people . . . will be over-borne, interpenetrated, broken down by an awful glorious sense of the encompassing presence of God. . . . We expect a real breaking down, here tonight, to hear sobs and prayers sweeping over this meeting." His peroration and prayer had an unmistakable touch of fire and as he closed, cries and ejaculations and singing broke out across the Tent.

To Hopkins and others the cries and songs had a professional touch: the Welsh, not the Holy Spirit, were turning Keswick revivalist. For thirty years one of Keswick's most blessed features had been quietness. But Hopkins, like Inwood, longed not to frustrate God's purpose.

On Tuesday an officially sponsored side-meeting gave the Welsh a time for exciting, factual descriptions of their Revival and that evening Hopkins began his address with a gently humorous plea for attention to "a little quiet teaching." At the Young Men's Meeting afterwards, during silent prayer, all kneeling, someone "began to cry out," says Meyer, "in such paroxysm of agony that no man, except two or three of that great number, dare lift his face from his hands to see who this sufferer was."

Next morning another incident, fervid, less melodramatic, changed the course of the Ladies' Meeting. A German deaconess, unexpectedly at Keswick to support an invalid brother, while sitting in the Eskin Street Tent attending Webb-Peploe's Bible Reading on "Peace" was "deeply impressed with the need of the heathen world which knows not this peace of God. . . . The responsibility of Christendom to take this peace to the heathen overwhelmed me. . . . But what was I to do? God had called me so distinctly to a definite work that I could not go." Sister Eva had founded on her father's estate in Silesia the deaconess home Friedenshort which sheltered orphans and incurables. "Then deep in my heart I seemed to hear the command, 'Give what thou hast.'" Her wealth had been made over to her Home; she was dedicated to a life of personal poverty. Her eye fell on her only two possessions other than clothes and necessities: her deaconess ring and an old silver Bible-clasp, of trifling material but rich sentimental value. "'Give your ring, your Bible-clasps,' I heard again and again." She fought the compulsion to stand up then and there, in all that crowd, to offer them to God. The Bible Reading over, Sister Eva hurried to the Pavilion, to find the Ladies' Meeting so packed (Hubert Brooke's Skiddaw Street Bible Reading naturally having stopped more punctually than Peploe's!) that she sat on the platform steps. Throughout Mrs. Hopkins' address Sister Eva heard the inward command to give publicly her ring and Bible-clasp "for the heathen."

Mrs. Hopkins finished. Mrs. Penn-Lewis rose. Before she could speak the crowd saw the German deaconess, distinctive by dress, rise too and in broken, almost inaudible English apologize, explain about ring and clasp, "though I know how worthless they are and I am almost ashamed to give them, yet I am obliged to obey the Voice." She sat down, drew a penknife and cut out the clasp. Mrs. Hopkins reached down her open Bible.

Suddenly she sensed movement in the hall. Someone came forward, drawing off a valuable ring. Woman after woman, young and old, brought up jewelry and placed it on the Bible. A girl of about twenty timidly advanced and said she had nothing to give but herself: "It has become clear to me today I must go out as a missionary." The atmosphere of dedication, in kind and in person, was unforgettable. And to Sister Eva the "most important factor" was her discovery that when, contemporary with the Bible Reading, the Ladies' Meeting leaders had gathered, one of them prayed "with great earnestness and faith that God would so speak to the hearts of His children that it would cause them to take their jewels from off their hands," to provide for missions.*

Frenzied youth, calmly courageous deaconness—they seemed to symbolize the forces opposed at this unusual Keswick. That Wednesday evening, after both tents had emptied except for a sprinkling of personal interviews, a group of enthusiasts hurried through the town throwing up windows crying, "All-night prayer meeting tonight, Skiddaw Street Tent!" Three or four hundred flocked in response, many supposing it official.

From the first Keswick in 1875 the Conveners had warned against edging out personal devotions by excessive attendances and late nights; should individuals or small groups seek the mountains, that was between them and their

---

* Sixty-eight people gave jewelry, and a few money. Friedenshort later sent sisters to China as Associates of the C.I.M.

Lord; mass meetings were strongly discouraged.

Yet here was an expectant crowd before an empty platform. The instigators determined that this meeting should be in the Welsh Revival manner, without human guidance. Several prayed simultaneously, loud voices violently and accusingly speaking in "what might almost be called a spirit of anger against the authorities because they would not turn the meeting into 'a revival.'" Pierson and two or three Welsh leaders set themselves silently to pray "that God would graciously overrule." Pierson mounted the platform. Backed by his known sympathy and the authority that an American accent often has for a British crowd, he said firmly that in nearby houses were a great many—some elderly or weak—needing sleep, "and any boisterous exhibitions on our part will disturb them." He was ready to stay till 3 a.m. "Those who want a quiet prayer meeting should raise their hands." Every hand waved.

Three hundred and sixty-eight written requests were sent up. Pierson read each one out, someone would pray, one and a half hours flew by quietly, followed by confessions from all quarters of the Tent, which had filled considerably; then a solemn witness of faith; finally, at twenty-five to three, praise.

On Friday came triumph. E. W. Moore molded the first address in the Skiddaw Street Tent around Paul's theme of the fire of judgment testing every Christian's work and character. He spoke quietly, the great audience in the hollow of his hand. As he reached his climax—a graphic picture of a burning house, clanging fire-engine, the owner saved by hair's-breadth—Pierson, due to speak next, "felt God's refining fire going through me, revealing the wood, hay and stubble of work and motive."

They sang the intermission hymn. Pierson ascended the rostrum: humbled and overwhelmed, he openly confessed. His simplicity, sincerity, moved profoundly. Without pre-meditation Pierson next begged those who "like me have felt conscious of God's direct dealing to stand with me before God, as those who here and now beseech Him to refine us." To his astonishment, the entire Tent rose. Pierson led in prayer, intending to follow with his address on "Praying in the Holy Ghost." But, as Webb-Peploe remarked, "God had no need of the address, as He proposed giving an illustration of the theme instead!"

Before Pierson could begin, a man stood and reverently uttered a brief prayer of confession. As the man finished, others were on their feet. For two and a half hours Pierson stood with no further movement than an occasional pointing if two began to pray at once. "Scores of people got up and confessed openly those things that had been a hindrance," recalls E. L. Langston. "I well remember one parson who said he was going home to burn up all his sermons—going to be a new husband to his wife, a new father to his children, a new vicar to his parish—as he asked God to fill the barren places in his life and ministry."

"No improper word was spoken. All was subdued, but deep, intense, searching. . . . It was quite obvious God had set aside chairman and speaker and was both presiding and speaking. There was a strange hush of God, and few, if any, loud outcries. . . . Few left the meeting, and meanwhile a great crowd gathered outside." They could have gone on far longer.

At last two hymns were sung, "and we quickly adjourned, with the profound sense that God had visited His people."

# Sixteen

## End of an Era

The Welsh were disappointed. "Keswick had not a little to do with the birth of the Revival," wrote R. B. Jones in his book a quarter of a century later, "and many have wondered [why] the nurse did not seem to welcome as heartily as might be expected what was in large measure her child." To the 1906 Keswick came the mighty Evan Roberts. On the last day in the Skiddaw Tent, when Meyer rose to speak Roberts rose too and prayed for him publicly, and later obtained leave to contribute strong words to the aftermeeting. On another occasion the young Welshman was invited to give a special address, "but he merely sat silent on the platform, and stood and prayed silently. The meeting developed into a rather hysterical prayer meeting, with people praying simultaneously all over the tent, and was finally made to conclude by the chairman."

Such incidents impressed, yet left a curious taste. By 1908 customary ways were restored: "There has perhaps never been a quieter Convention. No physical manifestations—no looking for spectacular evidences; no dependence on night hours or protracted vigils." The Welsh Revival subsided, like all revivals since the days following Pentecost, leaving a clear mark on Wales and its people. England did not blaze. Whether the Keswick Convention had misinterpreted its role is an imponderable of history; there may be significance in that Keswick continued service to the Church, while Evan Roberts suffered nervous breakdown and retired from the public eye for the remainder of his long life.*

Moreover, the years before 1914 did display a spiritual vigor, but this was seared from memories by the First World War. What would soon be called Modernism might not have dragged the churches into the trough except for the upheaval of 1914–18; the immediate prewar period, despite heated theological argument, was vibrant here and there with revivals: Assam, the Punjab, Manchuria, Korea, South China. Keswick was directly connected with some and a clearing house for all.

Keswick's sympathy with beginnings of the ecumenical movement has also been forgotten or obscured.

In the admirable symposium *The Keswick Convention,* edited by Charles Harford in 1907, several writers emphasized the contribution to Christian unity. "Amid the clash of creeds and strife of sects," wrote Harington Lees, future Archbishop of Melbourne, "it has been found possible, under the banner whose tranquilizing motto is 'All one in Christ Jesus,'

---

* Many would dispute this comparison. "Evan Roberts . . . fulfilled the dream of the devout by undertaking a ministry of intercession. He avoided publicity, and . . . resisted the most glamorous offers to return to the Methodist ministry. . . . He ended his days as he had planned—an intercessor." *News Chronicle,* January 31, 1951. Evan Roberts, a man of rare charm and spirituality, died at Cardiff, January 29, 1951, aged 72.

for men to forget their religious differences in their spiritual union, and to demonstrate to the world that the 'Unity of the Spirit' is a fact." Lees pointed out, perhaps with an eye to the history of the Brethren or of the Salvation Army, that Keswick had not suffered "the unhappy fate of some religious movements, [which] while aiming at a new bond of union [have instead] thrown down a fresh apple of discord and add[ed] one more to the already over-numerous subdivisions in the army of the Great King." Another writer in 1907 could truly state that "During Keswick week High Churchmen, Low Churchmen, Churchmen and Nonconformists find, if spiritual men, that things on which they honestly differ are as nothing compared to that living Unity in Christ which there asserts its preeminence."

Unity was a by-product of the limited, overriding aim, the Promotion of Practical Holiness. Keswick desired neither to unsettle denominational loyalties nor arrogate to itself the initiation of discussions toward formal reunion. John Harford, however, as Keswick representative, attended the first unofficial British Reunion Conference at Grindelwald in Switzerland in 1892, and when some seventeen years later John R. Mott and his associates who had built the missionary Volunteers planned the Edinburgh Conference of 1910—generally accepted as the key date of the ecumenical movement—Keswick's interest was unqualified. This was despite the Student Movement's own doctrinal divergence that led the Trustees regretfully to decline, in 1910, the delegation which in former years had held an officially sponsored side-meeting on the Tuesday afternoon.

The World Missionary Conference at Edinburgh, having ended shortly before the Convention, "was upon the minds of most, if not all of us." Many overseas delegates came on to Keswick, which by now always had a cosmopolitan air: "The coal-black African, the swarthy Southerner, the dark-haired Armenian, the fair, blue-eyed Swede, the alert Chinaman, the graceful Indian, all are represented." Robert E. Speer, American missionary and early Volunteer, was invited to speak about the Edinburgh Conference.

1910 was a star year. For the first time since the Student Volunteers had moved camp, university men were again under canvas. In the later intervening years small houseparties for undergraduates had been arranged, those for Cambridge by Stuart Holden's wealthy sister-in-law, of whom it was said that her invitations were more forthcoming for young men from aristocratic Trinity. By 1910 the Cambridge Inter-Collegiate Christian Union had emerged from the troubled phase in which it had nearly forsworn its past and the camp was both evidence of renewed vitality and encouragement for unashamed loyalty to Word and gospel.

A star year also because of two series (unfortunately simultaneously at midday) of addresses by the Canadian Jonathan Goforth and the American S. D. Gordon. "Mr. Gordon—the writer of those wonderful books—was here yesterday," the leader of the Oxford Medical Mission in Bermondsey had written to Albert Head the previous year. "He said a few words—some of the most inspiring I have ever heard. Crowds of people would be thankful to hear him. Could you possibly get him to speak at one of the meetings." The Trustees got him to speak at five. His whimsical, gentle, penetrating "quiet talks," his little interjection "Are ye listening?" and quaint phrases, held extraordinary power and by his *Quiet Talks* (*on Prayer*, *on Power*, etc.) S. D. Gordon remains one of the very few pre-1914 speakers widely read.* Jonathan Goforth, prime agent in the Far Eastern revivals, ascetic, "strained and spent under the burden of a tremendous responsibility," spoke at "white heat while he shows God's people their sins." Gordon and Goforth, contrasting in characters and sphere of service, were equal in impact, and for at least one hearer, a young Scottish chartered-accountant on leave from Singapore, it was "an address by S. D. Gordon touching on Sacrifice which helped me, and possibly my sister, to offer in due course for missionary work"— and thus sent him to join Mary Slessor of Calabar.

When the 1910 Convention closed, the Trustees took the unprecedented step of inserting a special minute recording that "The Convention was one of very rich blessing, the power of God being over the gatherings from first to last. . . ."

The ecumenical movement was rooted in missionary soil, and Keswick maintained strong interest in developments from Edinburgh. The Bishop of Durham and Mrs. Moule were hosts to the international Continuation Committee of which Eugene Stock was a member, at its first meeting in 1911. Again, to rectify Edinburgh's unfortunate lapse in refusing to treat South America as a missionary continent (a sop to Anglo-Catholics, who considered it the sphere of "our sister Church of Rome" and lived to regret their lack of realism), Campbell Morgan, Stuart Holden, Inwood and others rallied scattered missions into the Evangelical Union of South America; the name was adopted and the new Society formally inaugurated at Keswick in 1911. Two Conventions later the Trustees maintained the Edinburgh link by a rear-

---

* S. D. Gordon was on the Keswick platform once again twenty-one years later, in 1931.

rangement, unique to that year, of the Missionary Meeting: in place of the usual sequence of brief talks J. H. Oldham, secretary of the Continuation Committee, provided a long review of the world missionary situation.

The connection with Edinburgh was natural, for Keswick constantly strengthened its united missionary impact. In 1912, as the result of a suggestion from India, the Keswick Mission Council enlarged *Keswick Week's* free distribution, which had grown somewhat haphazard, into "an organized ministry amongst missionaries and English-speaking native pastors, catechists and workers in the various mission fields." Thus the message now reached far beyond those who could sit in the Tents, while the Convention itself remained a veritable "meeting for making missionaries," and of companionship and renewal for men and women on furlough, and even for discovery of spiritual power after years of barren service. Well might Eugene Stock, at the missionary reception in 1913, offer thanksgiving: "We look back and praise Thee as we remember how Thou has blest the world through this Tent."*

"Today, as it enters on its fortieth year, the Convention rejoices in worldwide appreciation, a fact which is not without peril."

The Fortieth Convention, quiet and crowded, ended ten days before the outbreak of war—the war no one expected

---

* In addition to the thousands of pounds which had been donated through Keswick for the deputations abroad, for missionary hospitality, and to support Keswick missionaries, a single gift of £2,164 came in 1908 from a Miss Hambly of Kew which she asked Webb-Peploe and Walter Sloan to distribute to missions of their choosing.

just then. As elsewhere in Britain in July 1914, the "sense of national peril that day after day kept the minds of the crowds at Keswick in tension" related to Ireland, where civil war seemed unavoidable. The European crisis had dropped from major headlines and did not obtrude into forward thinking at the missionary meeting; indeed, throughout the week "the missionary chord was touched by speaker after speaker. . . . Another matter which appeared and reappeared was Christian union."

The speakers at this unwitting end of an era were representative of past and future. Among them Evan Hopkins, greyed and a little stiff, his hand rather shaky, his speech weighted, solemn with age; Webb-Peploe, thin and most venerable, whose "mellifluous voice . . . has lost none of its timbre"; and Inwood, now sixty-three. F. B. Meyer and the Bishop of Durham, inhibited by his doctor, were absent. Among men of the future were Stuart Holden and the strong-voiced Russell Howden and the Baptist W. Y. Fullerton. And especially, giving one of the series of Bible Readings at his very first appearance on the platform, the thirty-five-year-old Graham Scroggie from Scotland. "The Trustees are heartily to be congratulated on their discovery of this diligent student of God's Word" was the verdict of old J. B. Figgis of Brighton.

The weather that high summer of 1914 was perfect. The Cambridge camp out on the lower slopes of Skiddaw saw no shadow of death approach, as young men dashed down for an early dip in the lake, then "a quick dress and over the fence for a quiet time among the trees of Latrigg." "The roll of praise which surges through the great Tent . . . searching and powerful addresses . . . out on Derwent Water in a boat of an afternoon . . . singing hymns in a secluded spot under Charles Alexander's leadership . . . then on to tea at Lodore and back singing across the lake."

Stuart Holden, after a great Friday night address, dashed away "by motor and night express" to join the *Mauretania* and cross the Atlantic to Northfield. The crowds who stayed over the Sunday before dispersing for work or holidays (many of them leaving happily for the Continent just one week before the outbreak of war) heard a sermon from Webb-Peploe. Neither audience nor speaker were aware how extraordinarily apposite Webb-Peploe's words would prove: "We are closing our Convention, but what a lovely thought is this: I shall never go forth alone again; I shall never be by myself again. I never am to face the foe without a rock to fly into, a salvation to be kept trusting in, a defense in the hour of need and battle, a refuge if there is a storm or a crushing trial."

# Seventeen

## Better Order, Wrong Turning

The crevasse that was exploded across the path by the First World War and its immediate aftermath was all the deeper for being contemporary with the end of the makers of Keswick.

Evan Hopkins spoke only once at the 1915 Convention —which was wet and so boisterous that the Skiddaw Tent blew down shortly after the Tuesday Bible Reading had emptied its attenuated audience of women, the elderly, war wounded and ministers. He missed 1916 through illness. 1917 had no Convention, in response to the national call to cut travel. When the Convention resumed in 1918, using the Pavilion only, he was again absent, and died in his sleep on March 10, 1919.

At the Convention of that year Bishop Moule of Durham preached in strength, but he died during the spring of 1920. Webb-Peploe, rising eighty-four, in 1921 returned once again to a favorite theme. "His message on 'My Grace is sufficient for thee,'" recalled a working girl forty years later, "has often returned to my mind and helped me very much in times of trial and difficulty. There was a terrific wind and it nearly blew the tent in. The speaker's voice became quite inaudible." That great voice had gone at last, and next year his colleagues "decided with very great regret that as Prebendary Webb-Peploe's voice cannot be heard by many in our large gatherings he should no longer be invited as a speaker." Illness prevented his attendance as an honored guest. In 1923, like his dear friends of long ago, Canon and Mrs. Harford-Battersby, he died at Convention time.*

During the war years, when thousands of Christians were proving the reality of divine enduement in the mud and carnage and carnalities of the fronts, or in stricken homes after fatal telegrams (and while Inwood, well into his sixties, braved submarines to serve as Keswick missioner in Egypt, China and Japan) the Convention made two advances, one of value, the other up a wrong turning.

The first lay towards firm administration, urgently necessary on the retirement of Evan Hopkins as Chairman in 1916. The Convention had muddied along in typically English style. The Trustees who had taken over from Robert Wilson were all laymen except John Harford, and were domi-

---

* Eugene Stock, who as virtual creator of the missionary side has the right to be called a maker of Keswick, lived until 1928, dying at 92. He wrote in the *Jubilee Souvenir* (1925) but did not appear on the platform after 1914. The last important survivor of the events of 1873–75 was James Mountain, composer of *Wye Valley* ("Like a river glorious"), *Tranquillity* ("Jesus! I am resting, resting"), *None of Self* ("Oh, the bitter shame and sorrow"), etc., and compiler of the original *Hymns of Consecration and Faith*. He died in 1933, aged 89.

nated by Hopkins, yet not particularly aware of it. Restlessness among speakers, whose only voice remained the customary annual meeting during the Convention, had been quieted by adding two further (lay) Trustees in 1912 to bring the number to eight. The Keswick Convention Mission Council, that overlarge body, continued to administer the missionary and overseas connection.

Hopkins left no obvious successor. In January 1917, Keswick leaders adopted a "Constitution" together with a "Twofold Basis" of doctrine; amending these terms in 1919 to "Method of Administration" and statement of "The Purposes of the Keswick Convention and the Teaching given thereat." The eight Trustees, who continued "to administer temporalities," and eight elected speakers, two retiring in rotation each year, formed the Convention Council "in whom all executive action is vested." Subcommittees were established for "Speakers and Program," and "Missionary." In 1919 the Council added a finance subcommittee and altered its own composition to include ladies. Until the next reorganization, therefore, the affairs of Keswick having passed from the casual to the crowded were guided by an unwieldy Council of sixteen men and women.

The Chairman was elected for three years. The first (1917–20) was Canon John Harford, the second (1920–23) William H. Wilson.

Wilson had acted as Secretary to the Trustees since 1901, and on his father's retirement had carried the oversight of the Convention's property and effects and the hundred-and-one matters of local organization. By 1918 he wished to hand his duties over to a younger man. The new Council thereupon decided to appoint a General Secretary; and in defining his responsibilities it took, not without due deliberation, a wrong turning.

———  ——  ——  ——

Back in 1903 a meeting of speakers had proposed a "paid secretary with a London office to act as a center of reference in the affairs of Keswick and in the arranging of local conventions through the country." The Trustees had compromised by appointing Captain F. L. Tottenham to "organize as far as possible or give advice and help," as an honorary representative, but Tottenham told Hopkins in 1910, "the post lapsed for want of remembrance and on account of independent action such as Llandrindod Wells and Buxton." Conventions were sprouting all over the country, and Trustees and speakers in November 1910 discussed for nearly two hours "the need of the Keswick platform assuming a responsibility for the 'movement' . . . which God has owned and blessed in a remarkable way during the past 35 years."

The matter rested until F. W. Ainley, a North London vicar who spoke frequently at Keswick, urged W. H. Wilson in February 1915: "Could not the Keswick Trustees bring it into their gracious work to initiate and encourage and maintain Conventions for the deepening of spiritual life."

Undoubtedly there were conventions, many of them unwarrantably advertised "on Keswick lines" or "Keswick in . . . ," which were far removed in spirit and intention. Often their chairmen, as Harries Gregory of Hove complained, "failed to grasp the meaning of a Convention. One openly said (not at a meeting) that he did not believe he could ever lose his irritable temper. One literally screamed at the Almighty and demanded the instant closure of the war, etc. Sometimes my heart has sunk or would have done so save for Divine Grace, *knowing* that the chairman (changed for each meeting so as to give all a chance!) was a leader of a worldly congregation with worldly schemes and enterprises." Miss Helen Bradshaw had often been present "where it was painful to hear the attempts to teach what was wholly outside the experience of the teacher. . . . At the offshoot conventions it is most important to have witnesses, not advocates."

Late in 1915 some twenty-five persons closely involved were asked whether Keswick should set up a London Office, complete with a list of authenticated speakers.

Several returned a warm affirmative, assuring the Council that such an office would be most expedient. Graham Scroggie thought it should organize overseas conventions and the deputations too, and "the Movement should have its own periodical." Barclay Buxton from Japan wanted to add "a central place of prayer where the burden of all the Conventions was borne before God."

Others doubted whether "the remedy suggested—the establishment of a central office with a salaried mouthpiece, etc.—would not introduce greater evils or risks than those it would try to correct." "*We* do not mean that we claim to have a monopoly of teaching on holiness nor a monopoly of qualified teachers on the subject, but would our fellow Christians generally take us to mean that, and we do more harm than good?" asked Luce of Gloucester. Canon Barnes-Lawrence said the same: "I think that 'Keswick' would be charged with boasting of *a special commodity not to be ob-*

*tained elsewhere*." George Grubb naturally disliked the idea of attempting to "impart the imprimatur of 'Keswick' orthodoxy to the affiliated conventions," and W. Y. Fullerton, Home Secretary of the Baptist Missionary Society, recoiled from making Keswick "appear like a business concern. . . . The proposal would tend to make the platform a close corporation."

No one precisely indicated that central control would be a step towards creation of a new sect or mission, but Harrington Lees of Beckenham, soon to be Archbishop of Melbourne, in warning of the dangers emphasized that "the parent movement has become more or less an *influence*, permeating definitely or indefinitely all the Churches." Strongest of all opposition came from the aged J. B. Figgis of the Countess of Huntingdon's Connection who foresaw a narrowing and hardening. "Is it not something like limiting the 'Holy One of Israel,' to attempt to draw up such a list at all? We have been blest and been a blessing; more *machinery* is not likely to add to that blessing—rather the reverse."

Such hesitations delayed any decision for nearly two years until the new Council had been formed and Wilson wished to retire. In July 1918 a Trustee, Walter B. Sloan, former missionary, then Assistant Home Director of the China Inland Mission and son of the Sloan whose address at Polmont had helped Moule in 1884, took up the appointment of full-time General Secretary with an office in London on John Street near Gray's Inn.

Thus Keswick, whose private status had been one of its most precious assets, enabling men and women of differing loyalties and varied backgrounds to unite for a distinctive purpose, moved towards being merely one more organization.

Sloan's personal influence was an unqualified benefit: he was a man of calmness, steeped especially in the thought of St. John, who combined mastery of public speaking, efficiency as an administrator, and sympathy in personal contacts. The affairs of the Keswick Council, however, began to assume the guise of a mission society or (in a phrase not yet coined) a pressure group. At Keswick 1922, representatives of fifteen local conventions paraded before the annual meeting of Council and speakers, and in the course of mutual felicitations were informed that "there are fourteen other conventions organized under the auspices of the Council during the year." By 1926 the total had risen from twenty-nine to forty, twenty-five having started since the London Office opened. The word "Movement" that the makers of Keswick had used sparingly, almost under protest, crept nearly into official adoption, as in the Council minute recording discussion on "the subject of the Convention Movement and the Revival Movement being associated together."

One worthwhile development outlasted the experiment of elevating Keswick into an organization: the formation, in 1921, of the Keswick Fellowship; as an informal bond between those who would pray, the Fellowship became a permanent feature. Less happy was the decision to hold, like any society, "a monthly meeting in London, with a view to maintaining the interest of supporters of Keswick." Regular London meetings had been an early activity of those who had founded the Convention and could not contain their discovery of the "open secret," but their object was hardly to "maintain the interest of supporters"!

It was no coincidence that in the early 1920s Keswick's influence seemed to weaken and narrow—that the fears of

Figgis, Grubb and others were being realized.

Mercifully, when the experiment had run eight years, Stuart Holden, now Chairman, developed serious doubts. He had been one of its earliest advocates and he does not seem to have detected the principle involved, but he told his fellow Council members that the idea had failed, expensively: "While there are a few exceptions (and these chiefly, if not entirely, Conventions whose local leaders invite their own platform without reliance upon our London Office, as e.g. the most impressive of them all—Portstewart), a large majority of Conventions held under the Council's auspices are quite unworthy as representations of 'Keswick.' They do not secure anything like united denominational support; they are frequently small and without any impressive influence on the life of the local churches; in very few places do they attract even the attendance of the ministers; and they contribute practically nothing to the expensive organization which we maintain for the purpose of providing them with speakers." Feeble conventions which "reflect adversely on the parent Convention" had best die a natural death.

Walter Sloan had built up a satisfying and valued personal ministry. He regretted the decision, taken in Council in December 1926, but in June 1927, the London Office closed.

# Eighteen

---

# The Age of Stuart Holden

The first postwar Convention, 1919, had worldwide impact because of its formative part in the founding of the InterVarsity Fellowship.

A Cambridge camp not being feasible or, in the opinion of ex-servicemen undergraduates, desirable, Mrs. C. T. Studd formed a houseparty of Cambridge men, with two or three from Oxford, in two large houses on the Heads. The numerically weak CICCU had courageously refused a pressing invitation to sink its separate identity in the doctrinally broad Student Christian Movement—at that time powerful in Cambridge, but, except for two or three of its members, lacking spiritual strength and vision.

The first days at Keswick were arid. Five men therefore met informally one evening for prayer in their boarding-house drawing room, and did not separate until two in the morning. Hamilton Wilkes of Oxford took off his coat and "hammered the heavens." Before they separated, Clarence Foster of Cambridge, afterwards a Keswick Trustee, could recall, "We had a very certain assurance that God was going to work in the houseparty. Indeed, when we stopped there was something of Pentecost in the room," including a pervasive joy.

"The blessing fell next morning," wrote Norman Grubb of Trinity, Cambridge, George Grubb's nephew. "The atmosphere was so charged with His presence that men were getting alone with God, having things out and coming back transformed." Then they disappeared in twos or threes into the woods and hills each night after the Convention meetings, and they went up to their universities that October with selfish ambitions withered and spiritual urgency recovered, and an overwhelming sense of the holiness of God had brought new standards of personal conduct.

During the Michaelmas term, when Norman Grubb was in his room at Trinity—having just read a letter from another of the houseparty, now up at Oxford: "God gave me the vision of the InterVarsity Fellowship that was to be. . . . I saw that not only must there be this witness in every university but that God was going to do it!" Grubb organized a small InterVarsity Conference in North London in December 1919. Keswick speakers gave Bible Readings and "Convention addresses," and the final evening was devoted to a missionary meeting. Next summer there was again a Cambridge camp. The InterVarsity Conference became annual too, leading in 1928 to the formation of the InterVarsity Fellowship of Evangelical Unions.

Grubb said of that decisive houseparty in 1919 that, without it, the refusal to be absorbed in the Student Christian Movement might have led merely to stagnation: "With the decision against reunion came Faithfulness: at Keswick came Fire."

In the garish, unsettled world of the 1920s—tense, unhappy in industrial strife, impatient with moral standards—there were several prominent figures of Keswick, together with veterans such as Meyer and Inwood, as well as lesser-remembered or more-occasional occupants of the rostrum.

Russell Howden the Anglican and W.Y. Fullerton the Baptist took a little innocent pride in preaching without notes, Bibles in hand, "perfectly at ease . . . before the great audience." Graham Scroggie, with his clear-cut analysis of Scripture and penetrating application of its truths, would give the Bible Readings no less than twelve times in forty-two years. "All his Bible Readings, which were *magnificent*," runs one memory, "were shot through with worship and praise as well as teaching. There were also delightful touches of humor which never spoiled the atmosphere, and an obvious understanding of human nature." His measured voice and somewhat stern mien masked warmth of affection. "He was a most brotherly man in private," recalls a Trustee, "and I much enjoyed his friendship. I think he had the driest and richest wit of any man I ever met."

Another Scot was Dr. Alexander Smellie, tall and shy, whose writings of devotion and scholarship were read far beyond his own denomination, the Original Secession or "Auld Lichts," the smallest then in Christendom. He had first come to Keswick unwillingly in 1913, thirty-three years after his ordination, for an experience much like that of his fellow-countryman Elder Cumming three decades earlier—except that Smellie already was humble and sweet-tempered, if burdened and defeated. He became a most attractive convention speaker and reveled in what he called "the Keswick ethos, the Keswick temperament," which he likened to the joyousness of St. Francis of Assisi. Smellie's blend of learning and simplicity would have served Keswick well in the later twenties, as his Memoir of Evan Hopkins shows, but he was plagued by ill health and died in 1923.

An American present in the audience in 1921 might have joined the Keswick platform had he not developed his own "ideology." Frank Buchman had visited the Convention in 1908 while smarting at ill-usage from the managing committee of the boys' hostel he had run in Philadelphia, and on Sunday he attended a service in the Methodist Church where a woman, Jessie Penn-Lewis, preached to a small congregation.*

"She unraveled the Cross for me. . . . I had entered the little church with a divided will, nursing pride, selfishness, ill-will." "I saw Christ on the Cross," he said half a century later. "And there came in my life a vivid sense of having experienced the Atonement. And I left that service with a consciousness of having the complete answer to all my difficulties." Like Robert Wilder some years before, he wrote promptly to ask forgiveness of those with whom he had quarreled.

In 1921, returned from a prolonged visit to Asia, Buchman had been living at Cambridge and Oxford nearly a year when he joined a Convention houseparty. "I heard Dr. Frank Buchman speak in the evening at the Officer's Christian Union," writes Thomas Hart of Glasgow, "and he gave an interesting talk on 'personal work.' He had a reputa-

---

* Buchman's own accounts place this experience at Crosthwaite, but no woman in 1908 would have been a Sunday preacher in an Anglican parish church.

tion of getting to grips with men, including university students, that others did not grip." The following winter Buchman founded what he later called the Oxford Group (also known as Moral Rearmament) and for a year or two some claimed that this would prove the modern model for Keswick. The later controversy, which raged when the Churches took the measure of the Group, did not obtrude at Conventions.

The most distinguished new personality was Bishop John Taylor Smith. Taylor Smith had been consecrated Bishop of Sierra Leone in 1897 at the age of thirty-seven, and by a set of curious chances became a favorite preacher of Queen Victoria. Edward VII insisted on his appointment as Chaplain-General to the Forces. For no less than twenty-three and a half years this tubby, serene, approachable bachelor bishop remained a potent influence in the British Army.

He had sometimes preached at St. John's on opening Sundays of pre-war Conventions, and had time to be a main speaker first in 1920. After his retirement in 1925 he came every year, unless abroad as one of Keswick's most effective representatives. He had the gift of the pithy phrase and apt illustration—and an inexhaustible fund of funny stories*—which held attention and flashed light upon spiritual problems and possibilities. His sway over simple minds, soldiers, boys, the young, was considerable, no doubt abetted by his swimming feats—including physical jerks and famous back-somersault dives.

---

* The Bishop reveled in stories against himself: At an early prayer meeting one Keswick a woman prayed, "O Lord, remove this modernist Bishop from our midst." The chairman, shocked, called out: "We will sing chorus number—," and gave the first number that came into his head. In a few moments, to the Bishop's delight, they were all singing: "I believe God answers prayer."

Taylor Smith was not an expositor so much as an excavator of Bible gems, to be noted in the wide margin and kept on the tip of the tongue. He was not in the least intellectual, with little interest in ecclesiastical affairs or politics, and towards clergy who did not share his convictions he was rigid, thus provoking considerable criticism during the war when the Chaplain's Department extended rapidly—until Kitchener solved the problem by giving Bishop Gwynne of Khartoum plenary powers for the Western Front as a Deputy Chaplain-General.

"Bishop Taylor Smith was dominated by one all-absorbing purpose," said his successor in the Army. "He lived only for one thing, the glory of God, and its corollary, the salvation of the souls of men." "Some of us remember," wrote E. L. Langston, "how during days in camp, at Keswick, or at some Quiet Day, whilst he was speaking, God brought conviction of sin, revealed our need of a Saviour, and searched us through and through." The multitude cannot be numbered whom he brought to faith, including hardened men who had been furious at his uncompromising exposure of sin. He was himself what he used to term "a skilled spiritual operator." "Bishop Taylor Smith," runs a report of Keswick 1924, "is always much in demand for personal talks, and again he found himself spiritual adviser to a host of young people. In fact sometimes he reached the meeting for which he started out only when it was nearly over. All along the way anxious and troubled souls had been waiting to seek his help."

The 1920s at Keswick were preeminently the age of John Stuart Holden, a man of great graces which brought many boons to the Convention, and of subtle defects which in the end nearly wrecked it.

The two decisive events in Stuart Holden's life were his conversion as an obscure young bank clerk of modest means in Liverpool, which led him up to Cambridge and then to take holy orders; and his marriage, in 1901 at the age of twenty-seven, to a rich woman. Jessie Galloway was daughter of a Glasgow shipping magnate who died three years later, leaving her extremely well off; and her heart and purse were unreservedly at the call of her husband and his ministry, first in parochial missions and a Keswick deputation to China, and then for nearly thirty years, from 1905 until his death, as Vicar of St. Paul's, Portman Square—which he did much to strengthen as an evangelical stronghold in the West End of London.

His was a very charming personality. Gracious and winsome and gay, with a strong sense of humor and a lightness of touch which brought a new note to Keswick addresses, he was greatly loved by all who came within his orbit. "His outstanding gift," writes his friend and successor Prebendary Colin Kerr, "was undoubtedly the gift of friendship. He gave you the impression, and with apparent sincerity, that not merely were you the one person he wanted to see, but that his time was yours. Added to this gift was his quite extraordinary memory for names, faces, and occasions. He had but to see you once in his church and maybe years afterwards in some distant part would recall that fact."

There was much of the artist in Holden: he was highly musical, and an accomplished, even brilliant, speaker who chose words from wide reading and a fertile imagination, with an acute ear for rhythm and clarity; sermons were as pleasing to read verbatim as to hear, and his pulpit voice "so soft that merely to listen to it is a pleasure, and so perfectly pitched that not a word is lost even in the far corners of the church." There was much of the businessman in him too. "Very particular about details," notes his secretary, "methodical to a degree." These traits were subordinate to the pastor in him, to the man of prayer and the preacher. Whatever happened later, there were men and women all over the world who were better and happier, and more fruitful in character and action, for having heard or read Stuart Holden.

The Holdens were childless and in a financial position rare among the clergy. Holden dedicated his means to the "one passion only . . . to pass on his Master's teaching . . . to bring his fellow-men to his own Saviour." He was generous with money and time almost to a fault. Wealth brought dangers. It was not that he could have a house in London and an estate in Scotland, a (secondhand) Rolls Royce and a chauffeur, but rather that money made him master of his destiny. Stuart Holden had power.

Holden was elected Chairman of the Keswick Council in July 1923, and in the next three years the Convention made notable advances. He brought encouragement and considerable publicity by organizing the Jubilee in 1925, a time of thanksgiving and rededication which reverberated around the earth. The same year he initiated Young People's Meetings, first in the Drill Hall, then in the Eskin Street Tent.

Meetings for girls had been held since early days, and for young men spasmodically before the First World War. A mixed Young People's Meeting (entry restricted to those under thirty) was an innovation as refreshing in the new age as it would have been unthinkable in the old. Holden chose nine to ten p.m. as the hour, and with youthful eagerness would join the crowd flocking across after the close of the main Convention meeting. "Holden started choruses (he could sit down at the piano and play them himself), testimonies, questions, etc., all very free and easy," writes Lindsay Glegg, the London businessman who later helped him, with Harold Earnshaw Smith, a missionary invalided from Nigeria, and others. Graham Scroggie one quiet evening was strolling on the slopes of Skiddaw with the Australian preacher Lionel Fletcher. "Lionel, we must get back quickly; did you hear that roll of thunder?" "That's not thunder, that's a roar of laughter coming from Lindsay Glegg's crowd in the young people's tent!" Hilarious or not, the Young People's Meetings were an immense blessing to many, including future Trustees, before they were capable of deeper theological thought.

The meetings quickly became a vital influence in deepening and clarifying faith and consecration, and an attraction which undoubtedly helped to raise attendance by young people at Keswick from about two hundred and fifty until well over a thousand. After Holden's day the hour had to be altered to the morning because too many would skip the main Convention meeting, the most important of each day, to save their energies or to secure good places for Eskin Street—thus, for all the aid received there, missing the Convention's full benefit, which is not listening to addresses merely but being part of a great company in mutual, progressive experience. Nevertheless Holden and the pioneers of the Young People's Meetings had established a component of Keswick almost as important as the missionary meeting.

The cohesion of the Convention, the mutually shared experience which had been one of the strengths of the early years, had been much increased when Holden persuaded the Council to a sensible retrenchment: in 1926, for the first time since 1901, the main Convention meetings reverted to one Tent.

The postwar decline in attendance had opened yawning gaps in the serried ranks of audiences, accentuating the tendency to flock to favorite speakers. The Skiddaw Street Tent was therefore enlarged for the Convention of 1926 to hold 3,200, a size made possible by installing, daringly, loudspeakers and microphones in the very year that the B.B.C. received its charter. The crackles and blurred voices at first blaring from the platform did not please every speaker: Russell Howden refused to start unless the amplifiers were switched off.

Holden next set his hand to tidying and rejuvenating the Convention office at Keswick, and improving conditions for houseparties. "The rapacity of landladies," he claimed in a confidential memorandum of October 1926, "and, in very many cases, the unsatisfactoriness of the accommodation and service provided was, this year, more evident than ever. Many and bitter were the complaints received. . . ." The householders of Keswick had once petitioned the Council for a more equable distribution of houseparties, their criterion apparently being the financial need of a landlady rather than the suitability of her lodgings. Holden's touch, however, soon set forward the efficiency of the Keswick office, and a happy relationship, now unquestioned, between town and Convention.

Holden moved the speakers from a hotel near the town center to the less crowded atmosphere of Castlerigg; in the older, smaller days they had been scattered among houseparties. A return to that custom being impracticable, he was wise to relieve them of the stares of the curious (the dining room had been right against the pavement. Watching Scroggie, or Meyer, or the Bishop eating soup was a familiar pastime for the idle). When Castelrigg Manor hotel came up for sale very cheap, Holden tried to buy it on behalf of the Trustees, as a going concern; mercifully his bid missed by a short head.

He urged, unsuccessfully, moving the Convention to June, to beat the local proverb, "When the Tents go up, the rain comes down." For various reasons the date was retained which had become established since the war: the third week in July.

---

By 1926, when Holden was reelected Chairman for a further three years, everything was going his way, almost frighteningly.

All warmed to his gracious, generous touch. Holden was a recognized pulpit personality of London. He had been editor of *The Christian*, he owned and edited another religious journal, *The Home Messenger*. He was Home Director of the China Inland Mission. He was an annual and highly acceptable visitor to platforms in the United States. He was the dominant influence at Keswick.

Had Holden reached his prime in easier times, the danger of such concentration of power might have been trivial. Unfortunately his lot was cast in a period which the perspective of history reveals as the nadir of Christianity in modern Britain.

# Nineteen

## Year of the Tattered Banner

With Biblical authority abandoned or denigrated by large sections of the Church, the principal historic doctrines of Christianity tended to be questioned, or adapted to modern ideas, or denied.

Keswick's own position was unequivocal. The Council assured an inquirer in 1921 of "their intention to continue on the lines laid down by the original Founders." The "Statement of the Purposes and Teaching given at the Keswick Convention" drawn up in 1919 made plain that the "personal experience of victory and consecration" which unites the speakers "naturally carried with it the acceptance of such truths as the Divine Authority of the Holy Scriptures; the Deity of our Lord Jesus Christ; His death on our behalf; His Resurrection and Presence; His Triumph and Reign." Maintaining these in an increasingly hostile environment, however, induced a defensiveness that nourished its own defects: evangelicals sometimes gave an appearance of encircled covered wagons, desperately warding off attacks of theological

Indians! Vision narrowed, and the defenders often adopted the posture criticized by St. Paul: "to measure themselves by their own standards or by comparisons within their own circle . . . doesn't make for accurate estimation."* Powder was wasted: more than once the Council sniped at Canon John Harford, the founder's son, and hinted that he should resign his trusteeship because they thought "his views and teaching concerning the Word of God were so entirely out of accord" with their own. Harford, a theologian of true evangelical convictions, declined the hint. The matter dropped.

Yet if defensiveness might tempt occasionally to spiritual fastidiousness, healthy discernment in such matters was vital. Stuart Holden's lack of it, his impatience with questions of doctrinal orthodoxy, his generous assumption that a man's sincerity could be enough, wherever it might lead, were storing up trouble for Keswick.

The defensive did not turn Keswick pietistic, as if holiness could be lived in a vacuum. Speakers and Chairman were not ignorant or unfeeling about economic and political problems agitating the nation, but critics or inquirers who sought pronouncements misunderstood the purpose of the Convention. In every decade, on every grave issue from the coal strike of the early twenties to nuclear arms, there have been those who wished to commit Keswick to a particular view or wished the Council to be an evangelical Vatican issuing authoritative verdicts. Since every decade the composition of attendance widens in background and nationality, for the platform to grow partisan would increasingly blunt its message.

---

* 2 Corinthians 10:12 (J. B. Phillips).

The defensive did accentuate possible weaknesses. In 1907, in a shrewd final chapter of the symposium *The Keswick Convention*, Dr. Charles Harford indicated "some of the dangers which may arise and which need to be recognized if they are to be avoided." His prescience was remarkably confirmed in the years following the First World War.

One lesser danger, inherent in all periods, is that of mixed motive. "The Convention has been compared sometimes to a great Spiritual Picnic," wrote Harford, "and many have gone rather with the idea of meeting with a number of pleasant Christian people than with the purpose of meeting with God; and . . . some go to further the interests of some branch of Christian enterprise." The bookstalls and booths which line the streets leading to the Tents are inevitable and useful but they can distract—and sometimes embarrass, as when a violent controversialist had to be asked to remove offensive literature. A worthy society might batten upon the Convention like some pious vulture: a very small, obscure overseas mission used to take a large house, fill it by advertisement, and require each member of the houseparty to wear an outsize badge as if a supporter of that mission; and a somewhat similar exploitation is the worldwide use of Keswick as a trade name, the plethora of Keswick calendars, almanacs, guest houses.

A more serious danger is if doctrine and practice do not coincide. Among the thousands leaving Keswick after a Convention there might always be those who would deny its message by their behavior, but the Council took pains to avoid inviting any speaker of whom it could be complained: "No man *talks* more about the 'Fullness of the Holy Spirit,' but no man *knows* less about it"; that their care was almost totally vindicated is one cause for Keswick's continued value. A chairman has commented privately, "Speakers may be subject to special Satanic attacks because of the message they proclaim, and speakers are no more perfect than anyone else: 'Let him that thinketh he standeth take heed lest he fall.' A deep and real humility is an essential prerequisite of effective speaking at Keswick."

The most serious weakness that emerged in the twenties had also been foreshadowed by Harford. "Many who know the early Conventions," he had written in 1907, "have felt that there is already rather less definiteness in the delivery of the message." Nine or ten years later this lack of definition had grown into a major defect. The thoroughly grounded expositions of Moule, Hopkins or Webb-Peploe were in the past. Graham Scroggie and Campbell Morgan were of Webb-Peploe's quality as Bible teachers but Morgan could seldom come to Keswick.

These tendencies reflected the general malaise of evangelicals, who had reacted oddly to the trend of the times by virtually fleeing from the Bible themselves; inroads of literary criticism had frightened them off scholarly exegesis, off theological depth and intellectual clarity. Keswick, for its full impact, needs a strong background of Christian doctrine; the Convention arose in a period possessing wide knowledge of basic doctrinal truths. It nearly died in a period of ignorance.

At such a time the Bible Readings become even more important. Holden wished to downgrade them. He was right to insist that they should "either be progressive exposition of the Keswick Message or should supplement it by illustrative Bible studies" and not be casual chats on Bible themes, but he forgot that to the founders the "Keswick Message" (the term they reprobated) grew out of the whole range of Christian truth, and he was wrong to suggest that the Bible Readings should take a subordinate position.

Lack of definition meant that Keswick was sailing towards the shallows. It might ground on one of three sandbanks.

It might become merely a general Christian conference at which uncoordinated good thoughts would be expressed, old sermons repreached ("This latter," Holden said, "has had not a little to do with the diffuseness and relative ineffectiveness of many Conventions") and the clear, limited objective of the founders be forgotten. Such a conference would quickly lose its point and stay alive only by vested interest.

The second sandbank was a narrow "specialist" view of practical holiness: Keswick would become dedicated to some slick panacea, as if acceptance of a formula, or a particular interpretation of a Bible passage, were the quick-mix recipe for Christian victory. And the third was dependence solely on emotional or spiritual experience. "The great fact that the believer may enter upon a life of holiness by a definite act of faith," Harford had written, "has led some to believe that the Christian life may be a series of new starts. Such people come to the Convention year after year expecting to get a fresh stimulant, as it were, to enable them to cope with the work in which they are engaged." The housemother of one party in the twenties used to retire to her room, once each Convention, for agonizing; and emerge to announce that she had "got the blessing."

Keswick did not founder upon any of the sandbanks but sailed perilously close to each. And when, soon after the Second World War, the Convention came under fire from certain younger evangelicals, most of whom had never attended, their broadsides were in fact ranged on the sandbanks and not on the vessel launched by the founders.

Nevertheless, whatever fluctuations could be detected, Keswick in the 1920s maintained a Christian gold-standard of sterling value in an age of depreciation. By the Convention addresses, by its influence on youth, by the nightly Open Airs which had their tale of conversions, among tourists and townsfolk, by the clarion call of the missionary meeting through which hundreds discovered or accepted their vocation, and by the strength and reassurance imparted to missionaries on furlough and their national colleagues, Keswick could be reckoned a major factor in world Christianity.

Sir Francis Outram, who for over thirty Conventions organized the stewards in their essential, unsung service, once wrote of a "wonderful fact. . . . From my seat on the platform, on the watch for any emergency, I have had constantly to scan the faces of the congregations. At the start of the Conventions, many a face have I noticed looking troubled, and ofttimes miserable; but as the days passed, how they brightened! And before the end were beaming with joy."

---

By 1926 some dissatisfaction was expressed in the Council under the leadership of Stuart Holden about the production by Marshall Brothers of the *Keswick Week*, the printed record of each Convention. Its editor was the Editor of the *Life of Faith*, a Scotsman called J. Kennedy Maclean. Holden, after interviews with Marshalls, wanted Keswick to found its own paper and also to publish the written record of each Convention. But for the Council as such to enter business would have been unfortunate, and providentially a subcommittee reported against the project.

At a Council meeting on January 30, 1928, at which (the Minutes state) "dissatisfaction was expressed with the contents of the *Life of Faith*," it was decided that any quasi-official connection should be terminated. Holden called on the directors of Marshalls and they agreed amicably. However, during the next weeks the *Life of Faith* printed an Open Letter to the Council, followed by articles, in which missionaries in Burma or Brazil were astonished to read a clear implication that the present leaders of Keswick plotted to betray it, that behind the threatened severance of the Convention from the *Life of Faith* lurked the fact that the Council, under Holden, was fast going modernist; the Editor of the *Life of Faith* called on his readers' aid.

Maclean brought to a head a widespread uneasiness that Stuart Holden's leadership was compromising the Convention's principles.

Holden had made statements, especially in America, which in that period of doubt and bitter theological dispute could not fail to cause disquiet. Thirty years earlier or thirty years later it might not have mattered if a man of Holden's previously recognized doctrinal position chose, out of friendliness, to share strongly liberal platforms or, out of generosity, to commend modernist writers, but when many preachers and theologians were abandoning earlier views of the Bible, Holden needed utmost care of tongue and pen if he were not to give the impression that he too had revised his beliefs. Impatience with definition trapped him into comments which upset many and worried those who loved and admired him. He scorned to elucidate his true meaning. He could not see that in the unhappy atmosphere of the times he was embarrassing Keswick.

Holden assured his fellow Trustees of his "entirely unchanged fidelity to the Divine Inspiration of the entire Bible as the Word of God," but the damage was done.

By the early summer of 1928 two battles were raging at once. The Council's resolutions, Marshall Brothers was told, "cannot under any circumstances be receded from as they constitute the considered judgment of the Council." The Council itself, however, stood divided over Holden's leadership. "Much as I loved Holden I was one of those who believed him to be at fault," recalls one man of moderate, balanced discrimination. And a second: "Holden was our very dear friend and we owed him much, but I still think he was at fault."

At the beginning of the 1928 Convention the Council members who feared Holden was damaging Keswick found a mouthpiece in W. H. Aldis, who approached Holden privately. Aldis, a member of the China Inland Mission, who since being invalided home in 1916 had served, although three years older than Holden, as his assistant at C.I.M. and curate at Portman Square, was no factionmonger but of deep charity and strict integrity.

Holden was deeply hurt that his own protégé should take the other side, and broke off all friendship.

Here lay the crux of the dispute of 1928. Holden saw the whole episode in terms of personal loyalty. "Dear man, he could not stand anyone or anything that stood in his way," recalls one of his colleagues, "and he was determined to get complete control of Keswick." It was highly improbable that Keswick would go modernist; the profounder issue centered elsewhere: should Keswick be an autocracy, dominated and directed, however worthily, by one man? Robert Wilson and Evan Hopkins in their time naturally held a special position; had Holden, as he imagined, succeeded to it, so that Keswick in effect was the private preserve of the Chairman, the Council carrying out his behests? Or should Keswick truly be led by an elected group having no sovereign but the Holy Spirit?

That year, 1928, the pennants flew over the Tents as before proclaiming *Love, Joy, Peace*, and the great red banner above the platform proclaimed *All one in Christ Jesus*. To those who knew, it seemed a tattered banner. The veterans F. B. Meyer and Charles Inwood were present—both to die before the next Convention—and Inwood, physically feeble, preached under the strain of "a spirit heavily burdened," his son-in-law writes, "by the lowering clouds which threatened to overcast the serenity and brightness of the movement." One Trustee remembers Inwood "speak with passion at Council Meeting, and say, 'Brethren, we are on the edge of a precipice.'"

There was no open breach at the Convention of 1928. The blizzard blew out. The official record of the Convention was put to tender, and awarded to Pickering and Inglis of Glasgow, who published it from 1929 until 1939. Marshall Brothers amalgamated with Morgan and Scott, amicable relations were restored between Keswick and the *Life of Faith*, and after Kennedy Maclean's comparatively early death H. F. Stevenson began in 1935 his long editorship, ensuring that Convention and newspaper should become firmest of friends and allies.

For Holden, the dream of dominance remained, but mutual confidence had been shattered. He failed in an attempt of 1929 to hurry the Council into accepting his scheme for reorganizing the cumbrous Method of Administration; this sensible reform had to wait until he had gone.* That October, on the completion of his second term of office, the Council elected a wise, impartial layman, R. B. Stewart. Holden, though remaining a Council member, arranged his annual visit to America to coincide with the Convention, which he never revisited in the five years before his death at the age of fifty-nine in 1934.

Yet Holden's final Convention as chairman, 1929, had been clear proof of an overriding Providence, and during it he who had indeed done much by speech and pen, by his fervor and his friendliness, made a last and lasting gift.

For the first time since the war there were large numbers of first attenders, of all ages. "As to young people, one meets them everywhere . . . their overflowing vitality has almost completely changed the aspect of the Convention." The Bible Readings were Graham Scroggie's soon famous series on "Christ in the Creed." At the Open Airs the inimitable veteran Scot, John McNeil, and the equally irrepressible younger Irishman, Willie Nicholson, "both of them rough-hewn men of the people," had the crowds laughing one moment, intensely solemn the next. The Missionary Meeting, moved to Friday morning, "seemed to mark the climax of the Convention," wrote R. T. Archibald, the children's missionary

---

* The Method of Administration was revised in 1932, 1945 and 1949 and has been adjusted in a number of ways from time to time since then, most recently, in 2004, with the appointment of a General Director.

on leave from India. At its end a number of parents rose to signify their willingness not to stand in the way were one of their family called. "And then came an amazing response from the younger men and women."

That night, fulfilling a long cherished hope, Stuart Holden presided at the Keswick Convention's own first united Holy Communion in the Tent, a simple service of undenominational form. To the last moment before this historic celebration of the Lord's Supper the Council had "no idea whether to expect three hundred or three thousand. But," recalls one of those who took part, and found himself, a Nonconformist layman, administering the bread and wine to a bishop, "nearly everyone came and the Tent was crowded. . . . It was a bold move on Dr. Holden's part, but it was richly blessed and has been part of the Convention ever since."

# Twenty

## Slow Climb in the Thirties

At the Diamond Jubilee Convention in 1935 (as also in 1925) representatives from conventions overseas highlighted the continuing harvest year by year of the seed sown in 1875 on the Derwent Water shore.

Keswick deputations continued to travel, if rather less extensively than before the First World War or after the Second. The volume of addresses went to the four corners of the earth; and this year of 1935 the Empire Service of the B.B.C. carried, for the first time, a broadcast from the Convention, which had been on the air the two previous years on the North Regional program.

Keswick certainly had circled the world. Without formal link or responsibility it was regarded as the source, direct or indirect, of scores of similar gatherings large or small, new or old, short-lived experiments or hardy annuals, in outposts of Empire and missionary lands, in Europe, the Antipodes and South Africa, while "If you look in the Postal Guides of the Canadian Dominion and in that of the United

States," the audience at the Diamond Jubilee were told, "you will find that there are two postal stations marked by the name of 'Keswick.' These are Bible Conference grounds beside small lakes in the woods. Yet it must not be thought for a moment that these centers are the whole of the movement for the deepening of the spiritual life in America—the distances are so vast." In fact, in 1935 more than one hundred and fifty conference centers could be listed where a friend from Cumberland would feel at home, and to "announce in America that a man has come from the Keswick platform is to assure him a wide hearing and to give him the confidence of people from the start."*

Some of the most significant Keswick deputations in the years preceding the Second World War were to Hitler's Germany and to Eastern Europe in 1935 and 1936. Bishop Taylor Smith, one participant of the second deputation, brought a special gift of sympathy and encouragement—as if he knew that the fellowship of Christians would soon be blocked again by war. Bruno Offerman, pastor of the Deaconness House Hebron at Marburg-Lahn, never forgot how the Bishop came up to him on the station platform at Keswick as he rather sadly contemplated return to Nazi Germany: "He waved his hand, exclaiming, 'O brother, I got a good word this morning from our Lord. It is this little prayer: Keep me, Lord, *humble* before Thee, that I might be *powerful* for Thee.'"

---

* This book was planned originally to mention most, if not all, overseas Conventions. It soon became obvious that the effect would be to lengthen and weight the pages and thus restrict readability and circulation. Readers out of the United Kingdom should be able to discover details about local Conventions from the religious press.

The climb from the trough continued. 1934 had reported the largest attendance since 1907, 1936 the largest ever—when a wooden annex designed by Major Mainwaring Burton, a civil engineer who was secretary to the Council and Adjutant of the Cambridge Camp, increased the seating of the Skiddaw Street Tent. Being a permanent structure it needed to be at the rear of the grounds, and the platform was therefore reversed, the main entrances now facing the audience instead of speakers. The weather welcomed the extended Tent by a storm which blew down part of the canvas and brought to a summary stop the Friday Missionary Meeting—the sixth such mishap in sixty-one years.

The Chairman in 1936, newly elected to succeed R. B. Stewart (1929–32) and J. M. Waite (1932–35) was W. H. Aldis, who, with a three-year break during the War, served until 1948.

William Aldis was in his mid-sixties, but had a touch of perennial youthfulness: "of medium height and robust build, with a quick, brisk step, a warm handshake, and a smiling face which fairly radiated health and goodwill." He had an uncomplicated personality, a sterling honesty and a hatred of humbug which made him outspoken at times, but was balanced by sympathy. He was a saintly man and a merry man, and without a trace of pride.

Aldis succeeded Stuart Holden as Home Director of C.I.M. in 1929, the first to be full time; he was also the first Chairman of Keswick to have had active missionary experience. It was as a Chairman, rather than as deliverer of full-length addresses, that he excelled. His blend of shrewdness and awe, his sanity and practicality controlled the emotional temperature and deftly pricked any bubble of pretension.

"It was never on the momentary flow of a spiritual crisis that he concentrated attention," wrote Andrew Macbeath. "The vision which had come during the exultation of a great assembly ought to become, in his view, the momentum behind a life which was henceforth geared for action."

Neither in his own nor in the estimation of anyone else would W. H. Aldis stand in stature beside Handley Moule, Evan Hopkins or Webb-Peploe. There were no giants on the platform of the thirties, though speakers incuded good men and true like Canon Guy King. King was noted for his brief talks at the early prayer meeting, and for his simple, if over-alliterated, Bible Readings. He was supreme at the Sunday afternoon Children's Service, which was "crowded out," remembers A. W. Bradley, "not only with children but with grown-ups who could not resist coming along to hear his unique talks. He used to ask the children (nearly all local) what he spoke about two years ago and what illustration he gave, etc., to which there was a ready and accurate response. To this day one meets grown-up Keswick folk who remember him and the addresses he gave."

No attempt was made to attract great names, ecclesiastical stars or popular preachers. The plea voiced every few years since Keswick first became famous, that representatives of differing schools, or names that hit the headlines, should be given a hearing, misses the purpose of the Convention. A man might be a diocesan bishop, such as Wilson Cash—several times a speaker when General Secretary of the C.M.S. and when Bishop of Worcester—or simply a Brother, such as George Goodman the London solicitor; the qualification is a basic understanding and experience of the truths specially set forth at Keswick, the ability to transmit them, and willingness to work in a team. Convention speaking is a particular calling within the ministry, a distinctive gift, which might or might not be held by a widely used evangelist, or a theological college teacher, a businessman or a bishop. Moreover some who are happy and glorious in the pulpit of a church crowded with three or four hundred people, or at a smaller convention, fail in the face of five thousand.

One vibrant voice in the later thirties rang out with memorable conviction—that of Donald Grey Barnhouse of Philadelphia.

After a brief contribution to the Diamond Jubilee he came from America as a speaker at the Convention of 1936. His addresses were afterwards published as *God's Methods for Holy Living* and had wide circulation. Barnhouse was a large man of inexhaustible energy, with an expansive personality and a great voice. He had a brain of high caliber, could absorb knowledge from innumerable sources on countless subjects, speak several languages, was widely traveled and possessed an exceptional talent for the graphic and often witty anecdote to illuminate his meaning. At that time, and for many years after, he was a pugnacious controversialist who demolished theological opponents with genial gusto. He had a good conceit of himself, which his friends easily forgave for the rich enjoyment of his company. His sincerity was transparent, his love for mankind genuine, and each day for Barnhouse was an adventure with Jesus Christ.

Above all, he was an expositor with a profound knowledge of the Bible who spoke with complete conviction. In an age which was expositorily lazy or scared, and nebulous or negative in attitudes and thought, here was a clear, unhesitant note of authority.

In 1938 Barnhouse crossed the Atlantic again to give the Keswick Bible Readings. His series on *Life by the Son* did not conform to the normal pattern of a Keswick Bible Reading but made a strong impact. Behind the last address lay a story that echoed similar happenings in the great days of Moule and George Macgregor.

Barnhouse had twice tried out the series in America, but had replaced the last of the four addresses with another, which "I brought to Keswick, expecting to deliver it on the Thursday morning. In the early days of the Convention I could get no peace about the fourth message, and finally, leaving the small Tent in the middle of the Missionary Reception on Wednesday afternoon, I went to my room with the certainty that I must prepare an entirely fresh message for delivery on the morrow. With a natural reticence which was almost repugnance I prepared a very personal message, which came to me with impelling force." He told, simply, unselfconsciously, what "walking with God" meant to him in a twenty-four hour period of his ordinary life. From the moment he described how he had discovered the way to go to sleep turning a Scripture verse into prayer, so that "soon He became more real than the inside of my eyelids" and the first waking moments of the new day were fresh with the sense of the last night's verse and of Christ's presence, Barnhouse took his audience through an experience which blessed them then and in the stormy months ahead.

---

The Convention of 1939 having been held in the shadow of inevitable war, that of 1940 naturally was canceled; it would have come at the start of the Battle of Britain. In November Aldis explored the possibility of a Convention somewhere, somehow, for 1941. "Whilst we certainly do not want to act hastily or in any way which might embarrass those in authority, yet we surely must not give the impression that these God-honored movements are less needed in days of war than in days of peace. We need to be quite sure that we are not acquiescing in what would really be a victory for the adversary."

The only practical answer was a "Keswick Convention in Print"—five special numbers of the *Life of Faith*, reprinted as a paperback by Marshall, Morgan and Scott who thus returned to their former service as Keswick publishers. A "Keswick in London," four days with three meetings on each in a central church, took place during the third week of July 1942, and another in July 1943. They were notable for introducing to the Keswick platform Fred Mitchell, the Yorkshireman who had sold his chemist's business in Bradford to succeed Aldis as Home Director of C.I.M., and for a great Bible Reading by Graham Scroggie on "The Sevenfold Blessing of the Spirit." A. W. Bradley reprinted it as a Keswick Fellowship booklet: "Thousands of copies of it went out and we heard of how greatly it had been blessed to many and how it had brought a new conception of the Holy Spirit and His work."

The Chairman of the Council for 1942–45 was E. L. Langston, rector successively of Sevenoaks and Weymouth, a man of great drive and initiative, who was at his best in these smaller meetings, and in happier times as a Keswick representative overseas. The flying bombs forced Keswick 1944 to make do with print, and the war in Europe ended too late for a return to Cumberland in July 1945; meetings were held in the capacious Westminster Chapel.

W. H. Aldis had again been elected Chairman and already was planning for the Tents to rise again. The War had broken the slow climb. In the uncertainties of the day some thought that Keswick might prove to have passed its prime.

# Twenty-One

## Crusades and Jets

The Convention returned to Cumberland in the wet summer of 1946. Restrictions, rationing and controls had nearly rendered this impossible, except, as Aldis said, for many prayers, the indefatigable labors of A. W. Bradley, and the cooperation of the local authorities and others. The aftermath of war prevented the erection of camps, but ensured, after a six-year gap, that nearly three-quarters of those attending were on a first visit. New too was the *Keswick Hymnbook*, replacing *Hymns of Consecration and Faith*. Nor were lacking links with the distant past: the Maréchale, ancient daughter of the founder of the Salvation Army, again held her unauthorized holiness meetings in the Methodist Chapel. Veterans recalled the day long ago when the Maréchale having refused repeatedly the Trustees' reasonable request that independent meetings should be foregone, Christian charity triumphed and Bishop Handley Moule and the obstinate Maréchale were seen walking down the street arm in arm.

A small houseparty of Cambridge men, with a few from Oxford and elsewhere, were mostly ex-officers rather scared lest Keswick prove a Hallelujah display. They soon discovered the Convention's tradition of steady practicability—and discovered Donald Grey Barnhouse. An immediate invitation to return to England for an evangelistic mission the next winter at Cambridge (at his own expense) was generously accepted by Barnhouse, who thus undoubtedly played a formative part in the almost startling postwar progress of the Christian Unions at Cambridge and other universities, which in its turn would bring several younger men of spiritual force and intellectual power to the Keswick platform.

That same Convention Fred Mitchell, who was cast in the mold of Charles Inwood, courageously used his first address in the Tent to unburden his soul on contemporary attitudes to social habits which he believed must compromise a Christian's consecration. In a true Keswick tradition, that a man must set forth, with utmost honesty, the terms of consecration as he sees them, Mitchell's social analysis was more detailed than usual from a platform aware that an audience of several thousands, from different backgrounds, denominations, lands and races, may genuinely differ in the specifics of worldliness. One month before the start of the 1948 Convention, the Chairman, W. H. Aldis, died suddenly at the age of seventy-seven. He had been the hub of preparations. The Council invited Fred Mitchell to take the chair.

He and other Council members said that throughout the Convention, memorable for the visits of Archbishop Mowll of Sydney and others over for the Lambeth Conference, they had "a very special sense of being kept by the

Holy Spirit." In the autumn Mitchell was elected Chairman. "I could easily be overwhelmed," he wrote to a friend, "when I think of those who have gone before me. . . . But believing the Lord has called to the office, I take it up." Each year he prepared months ahead, once spending a morning listening and watching at Bow Street police court because "so many of us Christian workers talk about sin without having any real touch with it." It was said of him that he "seemed to reach the summit of his powers" at Keswick. None could forget the atmosphere of his Bible Readings in 1951 on "The Lamb upon His Throne."

Fred Mitchell's chairmanship ended in the autumn of 1951, but he was to be a principal speaker at the Convention of 1952. In May, returning from Southeast Asia, where the China Inland Mission (Overseas Missionary Fellowship) had begun operations since the forced withdrawal from Communist China, he was killed in the B.O.A.C. Comet disaster near Calcutta. The recently installed Chairman, A. T. Houghton, and the Council, at Convention time again experienced a special sense of Divine aid.

———

Each of the past few years had brought increased attendance at Keswick—a token of widening impatience with weak-kneed defensiveness in individual or corporate religion. The belief grew that the power of God could sweep Britain afresh. In 1952 an officially sponsored side-meeting heard a report of revival in the Outer Hebrides.

In 1954 came Billy Graham's Harringay Crusade, making a stronger impact on London and the whole nation than the faith of the most ardent had expected. Many who were closely associated with Keswick were in the thick of the Crusade, and British organizers and the American team both recognized the prime necessity of deepening the spiritual life of those who had decided for Christ. Billy Graham openly acknowledged a debt to Keswick. Crusade converts, Crusade counselors, hundreds of clergy and laity whose vision had been enlarged by the previous months flocked to the Convention of 1954. The Eskin Street Tent was restored to its original size to seat 2,500 and for the first time for thirty years held simultaneous evening meetings with Skiddaw Street. Keswick vibrated with encouragement and expectancy.

Under the Chairmanship of A. T. Houghton, General Secretary of the Bible Churchmen's Missionary Society, who had been an Anglican missionary in Burma and but for the Japanese invasion was to have been consecrated assistant bishop, the Council met the demanding opportunities brought by the Glasgow and Wembley Crusades of 1955, and the new spirit of dedication abroad in the land, and the marked increase of the unity between Christians for which Keswick had stood nearly eighty years. The caliber of many of the addresses would have rejoiced Webb-Peploe or Handley Moule.

The full power of Keswick's authentic voice sounded in such Bible Readings as those in 1956 from Dr. Paul Rees of Minneapolis, an Associate of Billy Graham, and George Duncan's Monday night address that year on "A Peril of Spiritual Maturity." If in the Britain of the later fifties the momentum of national revival seemed to relax, whether because of a slackening of prayer, or because of opposition from powers in some of the Churches, or of affluence choking the Word, Keswick year by year rekindled a flame.

In 1956 the outreach of the Convention expanded by the use of landline relays.

A relay from the Tent to a hall in London, by Post Office telephone, had been suggested to the Council in the later 1930s by W. Llewellyn Jones, who recalled that Lloyd George had used the method to relay an election speech. Not unnaturally the Council rejected an idea for which public opinion was barely prepared. During the Greater London Crusade, relays carried Billy Graham's voice to all parts of Britain, and in 1955 Llewellyn Jones, now a clergyman in Devonshire, wrote to A. T. Houghton. Houghton was dubious, since attempts to relay from the large Tent to the small had proved, as the Editor of the *Life of Faith* remarked, "frustrating and disappointing. . . . I suppose that the psychological factor prevailed, the sense of being so near to the large Tent and yet not able to get in." The suggestion was ventilated in the *Life of Faith* and welcomed: in 1956 some fifty churches or halls up and down the country received relays.

The following year the number had risen to seventy-five, and by 1960 to one hundred and twenty-five places receiving G.P.O. relays for one night or more of the Monday, Tuesday, Wednesday and Thursday of Convention week, making a total audience at Keswick and beyond of over twenty thousand. Unfortunately the Post Office charges, which had to be covered by the organizers of relays in proportion to their distance from Keswick, rose steeply early in 1961, and numbers dropped down to ninety in 1962. "Nevertheless," the Keswick Fellowship pointed out, "there must be many large cities and towns which could have relays if people would get organized."

Relays offer a fine opportunity for interdenominational cooperation in a locality but need most careful organizing at the receiving and transmitting ends. A reliable public address system at the outstation is as important as the exact pitch of the piano at Keswick. Wise handling by the local leader, especially from the moment when the Chairman in the Tent says "Good night from Keswick, I am now handing you over to your local chairman," and switches off, does much to ensure that the relay be not merely an interesting broadcast but of spiritual value. Speakers at Keswick have to remember the relays. "The misuse of the microphone by a number of the speakers tended to spoil things," one center complained. "Thankfully only one of those who shouted was on each night, so we heard one address clearly and the quieter bits of the other."

Arrangements for relays brought a load of work to the Convention secretariat—distribution of literature, posters and hymn sheets, correspondence with local organizers, negotiations with the Post Office; in other sectors too the accumulation of business made reorganization imperative. The names of A. W. Bradley and his wife had been associated for long years with the honorary secretarial side and the heavy responsibilities relating to property. In 1960 a London businessman, D. Radbone Pippett, took over as honorary secretary with more extensive responsibilities, including the oversight of the Convention Office at Keswick, with its resident Registrar, A. Walton, who had succeeded on the death of E. A. Birkenshaw, Registrar for over fourteen years.

The relays presented one special problem. Although local organizers were urged to arrange four nights rather than less, many centers could not afford them—and where they could, audiences probably would not be identical each night. It was therefore hoped in some quarters that Keswick would adjust itself to concentrate the whole essential teaching of a Convention week into each night. Similar pleas are often heard among the many hundreds—perhaps thousands—who come in from Lancashire or Carlisle or more distantly, for a day or an afternoon. The plea cannot be accepted. Priority must be given to those who are present the whole week. "The *sequence* of teaching is vitally important," the Chairman would stress. "This is the special gift that God has given to Keswick."

Relays can only be fragments of a Convention but their value has been proved. "Definite deep work was done," one center reported. "Many expressed how humbled and sobered they had been." "No visible results," reported another, "but a definite heart searching and stirring among Christians of all denominations. . . . This relay was supported by Anglicans, Methodists, Salvation Army, Baptists, Congregationalists and Brethren, as well as independent missions." "More young people attended and were very impressed. The tremendous challenge of Monday night will never be forgotten."

———— —— —— ——

The jet age enabled Keswick to fulfill ever more widely in a shrinking world its object "to deepen the spiritual life of all races and denominations. . . ."

Interchange with the United States grew closer. Only six of the seventeen Conventions between 1946 and 1962 lacked an American speaker: Barnhouse, six times before his death in 1961, Paul Rees, William Culbertson of Moody Bible Institute and Wilbur M. Smith of Pasadena. Keswick deputations circulated more widely. India illustrates, as one clime among many, the strengthening imparted to missionaries and national Christians.

Back in the late 1930s an attempt by several Indian Conventions, North and South, to pool resources and bring out a speaker from England failed because of expense. The vicissitudes of war and Partition enfeebled the Indian conventions. They were "in low water spiritually," writes the Secretary of the Nilgiri Hills Convention in South India, T. J. Brinicombe, "my own feeling being that they were too exclusively subjective and introspective. Attendances and interest fell considerably, and committee members were gravely concerned. In 1953 they passed a resolution that 'in future only those acquainted with the Keswick message and who were in a position to present it, be invited to be speakers. . . .' The committee felt that in the past two years the Convention had got away from its original idea."

Two of the Nilgiri committee, when in England, discussed their problem with members of the Keswick Council; and in 1955, as a cooperative venture of Keswick, the (British) Evangelical Alliance and the Evangelical Fellowship of India, George Duncan made a cold-weather tour of India and Pakistan, speaking at Conventions to considerable audiences of missionaries and nationals. It had been intended to repeat the arrangement every second year, but the response was such that one came every year from 1955. Keswick could rejoice in that deputations, not only to India but elsewhere, did not need always to be supplied by the Council. Men from Australia, New Zealand and America could be drawn on; significantly, each of them had been Keswick speakers.

George Duncan became one of Keswick's hardest worked representatives. His itinerary for the first six months of 1958 is an indication of the spread of Conventions around the world. Arriving in Sydney from England on Christmas Day, 1957, he spoke at the Belgrave Heights Convention near Melbourne, and elsewhere in Australia, before moving to New Zealand for February. In March he was again in the United States, which he had visited the previous October for the "Mid-American Keswick" founded by Alan Redpath, the Englishman who was then pastor of Moody Church, Chicago. "Mid-America" sought to follow Keswick more closely than did the Bible Conferences or Conventions usual in America, by restricting length to a single week or ten days, limiting its objective, and by teaching in deliberate sequence. From America Duncan flew to South Africa, Rhodesia, Kenya and Uganda.

A steady stream of invitations reached the Keswick Council from all over earth. India's comment, in the words of Brinicombe of the Nilgiris, is typical: "The sending out of Keswick speakers has revitalized our Conventions and raised the standard of ministry greatly. We have able men, and Spirit-filled men, amongst the missionaries in India, but so often such men are in need of spiritual refreshment themselves. . . . Blessings received are multiplied back in the mission fields."

*Keswick Week* remained a potent morale-raiser for missionaries and lonely Christians. Months after first recipients had opened the postal packet, dog-eared copies would circulate in hospitals and homes from the Arctic to the equator, wherever English could be read. And wherever English might be heard, the annual broadcast on the B.B.C. overseas service reached an enormous audience. It has been rated by the B.B.C. as Most Popular Religious Feature of the year, missionaries and those who have been to Keswick comprising a mere fraction of the listeners.

In 1957 the Keswick Fellowship established a tape library. Recordings of the addresses and the Bible Readings were offered on loan. By 1963 nearly fifty tape libraries had been established throughout the world. At the end of every Convention a complete set goes to each honorary librarian, who loans one or more tapes as required, no charge being made, but refund of postage being invited and—with that casualness which is seldom recognized as a negation of "personal, practical holiness"—too often forgotten, thus placing an unnecessary burden on the individual librarians abroad or the Convention treasury in the United Kingdom.

The Missionary Meeting is recorded too. The value of this tape to churches seeking a striking means of proclaiming Christ's demand that men and women should go to the ends of the earth for His Name has barely been explored; an imaginative minister with a Keswick Missionary Meeting tape, and well-arranged color transparencies borrowed from societies or embassy information departments, could make an unforgettable and compulsive evening for his people.

The Missionary Meeting tape can have also an influence on Christian unity. The days have long gone when the six-minute messengers were all British, save an occasional "native Christian." In 1962, among thirteen speakers were a

North Indian and a South Indian, a Vietnamese, a Japanese, and a Spaniard. The impact of such a meeting, the brief talks, the prayer and Scripture reading, the hymns and the Chairman's closing words, can be as strong in Singapore or Sudan, Durban or Demerara, strengthening cords of love and understanding, provoking prayer, enlarging the vision of isolated or introspective Christians.

This unity—demonstrated and enhanced by the tapes, as also by *Keswick Week* and the overseas broadcast—has been part of Keswick for over eighty years. The Convention and the ecumenical movement, however, had grown apart since 1910, and it was not until the early 1960s that they again drew nearer. At the New Delhi Assembly of the World Council of Churches, the Convention Chairman, A. T. Houghton, in his capacity as a missionary leader, was a delegate—and Archbishop Gough another. Among Keswick speakers, past or future, at New Delhi was Paul Rees, with Billy Graham; and one of the six newly-appointed Presidents of the W.C.C. was Sir Francis Ibiam, the Nigerian doctor and statesman who with his wife had attended Keswick in 1960.

Long before Edinburgh in 1910, through to New Delhi and beyond, the Convention could fairly claim to have been (in Houghton's words) "the most practical demonstration of real unity that is to be found in a divided, sinful world. Not in the boastful attitude of the Pharisee, but in the sincere recognition of unworthiness such as characterized the Publican, we humbly thank God that the motto 'All one in Christ Jesus' is not only preached but lived out in the atmosphere of Keswick, where denominational, racial, linguistic and cultural barriers are entirely broken down and a true unity of the Spirit demonstrated."

# Twenty-Two

## Prelude to Power

At the start of one of the Conventions of the 1960s, an American couple on board ship returning via Liverpool from a missionary term in West Africa happened to tune in to the broadcast. They had never heard of Keswick, but on landing at Liverpool they rented a car, drove straight to the Lake District, and were in time for the closing services. After that they continued to the United States for furlough and subsequently went back to West Africa.

Their story dramatized that the Keswick Convention is a point on a circle. People come in from Christian service, or Christian discipleship, and go out renewed, recommissioned. Were Keswick ever to break the circle and usurp the center—become an end in itself—it must wither and die.

The beauty of the unchanging lake and hills, in sunshine and storm, assists continuity through the decades. A veteran revisiting after forty years would be at home. And could the founders or their successors walk again on Friars

Crag or Skiddaw, where the sound of cars and stench of diesel-powered trucks is swallowed by the peace and freshness of the hills, they would rejoice. The words of Harford-Battersby and Wilson in 1875 still sum up the Convention's purpose: that Christians "may be brought to enjoy more of the Divine presence in their daily life, and a fuller manifestation of the Holy Spirit's power." Handley Moule's definition still sums up the message: "Christ *for* us on the Cross, as our peace with God . . . Christ *in* us for our emancipation from the tyranny of self, for the conquest of temptation, for the power 'to walk and to please God' . . . Christ *over* us, the Master, by every claim of lordship, sovereignty and possession." And, of Keswick's third generation, Graham Scroggie's testimony a few years before his death still sums up the significance: "There are multitudes of Christians who do not know Christ as Lord, as Master of the whole life; and if I understand the innermost significance of the Keswick movement, it is to expound this matter and to press it upon those who attend."

The full savor of the Convention can be known only in person, as the cars and coaches and motorcycles stream in on the opening Saturday to find, as a journalist wrote, "the strange sight of a town captive to the gospel for a full week, whole streets cluttered with the booths of missionary and other Christian societies, the shops full of Christian books, magazines and wall cards." In fields around the town are the camps. The two InterVarsity Fellowship camps in 1962 each held a hundred and sixty—the men's, successor of the pre-war Cambridge Camp, being commanded by a retired major of the Brigade of Guards (with ramrod back and military mustache) widely known in universities as an effective evangelist and counselor. The Boys' Brigade camp, however, could parade under a retired major-general, their national Brigade Secretary being also the Keswick Convention Treasurer.

A first-time visitor at the opening Saturday night cannot fail to be moved by the mass of people united in worship, by the reverent singing of many thousand tongues, by the rank upon rank of faces looking toward the flower-banked platform beneath the great red motto-banner. The Tent was further enlarged in 1960 by extending the wooden annex and lightening it with Perspex windows. Closed-circuit television (hence the strong lights and the spotlight which can be a trifle of a trial to a speaker) was installed between the Tents, thus eliminating the inconvenience of holding two simultaneous meetings yet providing space for nearly seven thousand hearers; a further gain being that the smaller (Eskin Street) Tent with the TV sets allows more detachment. A man or woman facing tumultuous issues, yet too conscious of the sheer impact of the meeting or the speaker's personality, may choose Eskin Street, to listen and watch more freely.

From the Sunday right through the week, the Convention is a unity in which atmosphere, activities and addresses each contribute to the limited but vital objective.

The early prayer meetings at seven a.m., in the fresh beauty of a lakeland morning, or in mist or drizzle, have a charm of their own. The benches are less packed, though many hundreds come, and with hymns, a brief talk, and prayers one after another from here, there and everywhere in the Tent, the hour moves quickly, even if sometimes an unthinking participant lowers the temperature by praying too long. In Eskin Street the missionary prayer meeting (from Monday to Friday) has unique force, for each country or area has intercessors with intimate knowledge and genuine concern: the concentration of prayer during that week must in itself be a major annual contribution to the Church's work in a world of ferment and need.

Before the Bible Reading at ten, the sight of streets filled with walkers converging on Skiddaw Street carrying Bibles would provide the casual bystander with a startling Christian evidence, and inside it seems the great days of Moule and Webb-Peploe are back. "To say that this was expository preaching at its best," wrote a Church newspaper of John R.W. Stott's series on 1 Corinthians 1–6, "is hardly to do justice to the immense vigor, fire and love for Christ and His Church. . . . Nor can it quite convey the impression of a man 'under' God's Word, using great gifts to unfold the precise meaning and application of almost every phrase. . . . Mr. Stott gave the perfect justification for such a Convention as Keswick in his persuasive demonstration of the fact that right action depends upon right belief; that ethics cannot be divorced from doctrine."

The mid-morning break (catered by a contractor from Carlisle) is followed by a Convention Meeting in the big Tent, and on the Tuesday, in one of the town churches, the Ministers' Meeting—often a formative experience. Simultaneously on four mornings the gates of Eskin Street are guarded by eagle-eyed stewards to bar over-thirties. The emphasis at the Young People's Meeting is on singing, from a special chorus sheet; instruction in which clarity blends with practicality; and personal counseling afterwards where sought. Younger members of the speakers' party generally are in charge, but one older man—whose "melodious voice, well-stocked mind and rich fund of humor" made him a most popular leader before his sudden death in December 1960—was the Principal of Oak Hill, L.F. E. Wilkinson, of whom *The Times* wrote that he would "be remembered as one who in a quite extraordinary degree radiated happiness and confidence. Those who knew him intimately for many years never knew him to be flustered or irritated or ever heard an angry word from him."

The afternoon Convention Meeting is arranged primarily for the day visitors, and, unless the rain is hard, a big part of the resident thousands scatter to the hills for drives or walks, or across the lake. Many missionary societies organize a picnic some day of the week for their members, candidates and friends; and once upon a time several boating parties about to embark, including a big missionary picnic, were driven back to shelter by a heavy shower. "The rain ceased, the parties reassembled, collected their picnic teas, and spent a happy afternoon. A party of Cambridge men were particularly delighted with the more-than-ample supply of cakes which, it seemed, a generous landlady had provided. Imagine their feeling when, on their return, they were met by the rueful band of missionaries whose tea had been—to say the least—sketchy!"

The holiday, open-air atmosphere is an aid to the Convention's objective. So too, for that matter, is the Open Air evangelistic service in the Market Place, from a platform raised near the ancient Moot Hall with its white walls edged by black, and the modern Woolworths, the banks and Ye Old Friars Cafe. The organizer arranges different teams to give testimonies, and someone to sing or play. Crowds flock down as the Tents empty but there is always a good sprinkling of strangers: youths lolling outside the coffee bar; a middle-aged man listening, puzzled, smoking a cigarette; hikers, townsfolk. In 1925 a missionary on furlough from West Africa asked a bystander if he would accept Christ, and for answer had a blow in the face. That night the missionary's houseparty prayed. Next evening in the Tent the missionary became aware, as he listened to W. Y. Fullerton, that the person in the next seat was in spiritual distress; he turned and saw the fellow who had hit him. They talked afterwards and the man gave his heart to Christ.

"It is in such an atmosphere," runs the confidential Notes for Speakers, "where love and unity are paramount, that the Holy Spirit is pleased to work in the hearts of speakers and hearers, and blessing flows out."

The earlier addresses "are expected to give a solid background of Biblical teaching on the theme for the day, and these should lead up to the challenge for decision and action at the evening meeting. Each day's theme builds on the previous, experience having proved that where the sequence has been forgotten or ignored there seems to have been less effective spiritual result, as far as human judgment of spiritual issues is possible." It is recognized that God may overrule. The climax may not come at the end of the week: "the testimonies of those who have received blessing point to the sovereign action of God, speaking through various means and at varying times, and sometimes outside the public meetings altogether." Indeed, the Convention would be meaningless except in the context of human need matched by Divine power: that in reality, as in the belief of speakers and organizers, the Holy Spirit is active.

And so, on the Friday, another Convention reaches the great Missionary Meeting.

The positiveness of Christianity, the compulsion of its outreach to the ends of the earth, have been inherent from the start by the very presence of the multitude of missionaries, most of them guests of the Hospitality Fund, and overseas visitors. At the Overseas Reception on Wednesday afternoon bright-colored saris and African robes splash the Eskin Street Tent, and the hubbub of renewed acquaintance and the clink of tea cups precedes the official welcome, the roll call of countries, sixty and seventy or more. Before that, a little committee, meeting two nights in a tiny room of Convention Lodge, has sorted out the lists and selected speakers for the Friday, whose words may direct decisively scores of lives as, one by one, in a gripping two hours, they spotlight the need and the Great Commission.

The last hymn sung, the Chairman rises. In measured tones he draws the audience to consider the implication of what they have heard. "If your heart and mind have been stirred, what remains? Your will. No one will force you to respond against your will. Are you willing to come in on this great task? The Holy Spirit may lay His finger on the part you need to be willing about." It might be the pocket, or prayer, or parents' willingness for their children to offer for service.

The Chairman then directs his words especially to young people: "Can you face the challenge of this meeting and make no response? For the majority, the call may be to work in the homeland. The Church of God is in desperate need of more whole-time workers. Ask God personally where He wants you to serve Him. Are you willing to stand and declare that you respond to the call to serve Him in whole-time service at home or abroad? Consider the thin red line of missionaries, in contrast with the millions living and dying without Christ. Will you stand to declare your intention by God's grace to serve Him wherever He might appoint? . . . While you are standing, we will pray that God will bless your determination, and the surrender of your lives."

That night, in the aftermath of dedication, the week of renewal ends in the united service of Holy Communion, seven thousand persons of every kindred, and tongue, and people, and nation, all one in Christ Jesus.

# Twenty-Three

# The Keswick Story Continued

*by Ian Randall*

The four decades since J. C. Pollock completed *The Keswick Story* have seen massive changes in British society, and, within that, in religious belief and practice. The 1960s, according to Callum Brown in his book *The Death of Christian Britain* (2001), saw the Christian-centered culture that had conferred identity on the people of Britain being rejected. The decade was a turning point in a number of ways. The postwar austerity of the 1950s gave way to greater affluence. The religious world in Britain was rocked by Bishop John Robinson's provocative book *Honest to God*, published in 1963, which called for a new understanding of God. 350,000 copies of this book were in print within a year. In the same year Beatlemania was reaching its height. A widespread desire for authentic spiritual experience was also evident. Ecumenism was a growing force within the ecclesiastical world. The Keswick Convention, along with wider evangelicalism in Britain, was faced with new challenges. New features became common in evangelical life that had not been part of the traditional Keswick ethos, and the Convention, with its long and proud history, at times in this period found it hard to adapt. New Christian events that were launched in these decades in part drew (often very significantly) from Keswick, but because they were new they were free to operate in new ways. Ultimately, however, Keswick has not only survived but has flourished.

---

From the mid-1960s the thrust of the Convention's historic teaching about holiness in relation to deeper spiritual experience became a matter of debate. John Stott, who was very well known and respected for his outstanding expository ministry from the 1950s at All Souls, Langham Place, London, spoke at Keswick for the first time in 1962, giving the Bible Readings in that year. The *Keswick Week* reported that the main characteristic of the meetings that year was exposition of Scripture, directed more to the mind and will than to the emotions. Stott's Bible Readings were widely regarded as masterly, setting the tone for the whole Convention and being seen by some commentators as ranking among the greatest utterances ever delivered at Keswick. But Stott's approach to the spiritual life was somewhat at odds with traditional Keswick teaching about an experiential freedom from the power of sin, and Stott provoked considerable controversy when he returned to the Convention in 1965 and expounded Romans chapters 5–8 in the Bible Readings. In these addresses Stott explicitly countered common ideas in evangelical spirituality, such as the idea of progressing in

Christian experience from the struggles of Romans chapter 7 to the victory of chapter 8. The Keswick teaching of the past had given great prominence to the call to believers to come to a point of surrender in their Christian lives in which through the Holy Spirit they knew victory over sin.

The evening meetings at Keswick in this period reflected the belief that there was such progression. Drawing from the older Keswick concept of the Convention as designed primarily to be a place of encounter with God, the teaching from Sunday through to Friday followed a sequence. On Sunday the theme was the spiritual inheritance of the Christian; on Monday, sin in the life of the believer and the call to repentance; on Tuesday, union with Christ in His death and resurrection, and freedom from sin's guilt and power through faith; on Wednesday, the Lordship of Christ and the call to yield to Him for victory over sin; on Thursday, the ministry of the Holy Spirit in the life of the believers; and on Friday, the challenge to live out the new life in the world. This scheme continued, with some degree of flexibility, into the 1990s, when a specific theme for the Convention week was introduced. The consecutive morning Bible Readings were intended to enable the theme to be covered. This moved the Convention away from the traditional Keswick sequence of teaching. This move reflects the fact that the emphasis of John Stott and other influential speakers at Keswick from the 1960s onwards—such as Eric Alexander (who became a leading Church of Scotland minister) on Biblical exposition being paramount—has replaced the earlier Keswick thinking about the centrality of the challenge to enter into the experience of holiness by an act of consecration.

In the 1960s, however, these issues still provoked intense

discussion. The minutes of the Convention Council make reference to concerns about John Stott's expositions and Biblical interpretation for more than two years afterwards. Debates took place not so much about *victory* (this was already less prominent as a theme at Keswick), but about what it meant to *die to sin*. In his exposition of the crucial chapter, Romans 6, Stott challenged the view that the Christian was being told in that chapter to reckon the old sinful nature as dead through a *conscious act*. Stott mentioned commentators who took this approach, but argued that there were *fatal objections* to it. For Stott, death to sin took place in Christ's taking the penalty of sin on the Cross—and in this sense the Christian, by his or her union with Christ, also died to sin. In Jesus Christ, said Stott, "we did die—not in our own person: that would have meant eternal death—but in the person of Christ our substitute. . . ." As a result the old life, for the believer, was finished. The emphasis in Stott's exposition was on the death of the old self at *conversion*. The biography of a Christian, he suggested, was written in two volumes. Volume 1 was the story of the old self, before conversion. Volume 2 was the story of the new self, after being made a new creation in Christ. The secret of holy living, for Stott, was in the Christian's renewed *mind*. It was in knowing that "our old man was crucified with Christ" (v. 6).

At the 1967 Convention, however, Alan Redpath, the founder of the Mid-America Keswick, gave an evening message on Romans 6:6 which struck a traditional Keswick note. Redpath had been present at John Stott's studies in 1965 and had been deeply unhappy. "We are not gathered here in a 'happy little holiness huddle' which isn't relevant to these critical days," Redpath pronounced in 1967, "we're here to see how the Church can recover her lost power and vitality, and once again become a dynamic force which could sweep through this twentieth-century materialism, sin and opposition in sheer defiance of the gospel. But that can only be done by Christian people throughout the world who are living in the joy of full salvation." He then put forward the view that freedom from sin's dominion was "a blessing we may claim by faith." He argued that the Convention was founded to declare this truth and that "we are in this tent this evening in order that we may enter in by faith to an experience of deliverance from sin's tyranny, as vital and real as at our conversion when we received Jesus Christ as our Saviour and entered into the joy of forgiveness of sins. *Deliverance* from sin, as well as forgiveness for our sins, was provided at the Cross." The *Keswick Week* reported: "Mr. Redpath invited those who wished to make this transaction with the Lord to stay behind, and well over five hundred did so. After further instruction he asked those desiring to commit their lives to the Lord to stand, and more than half stood and said after him an appropriate prayer. Evangelist and the pastor have combined in Mr. Redpath for this ministry of leading Christians to the place of total commitment to the Lord and thereby trust in Him for *full salvation.*"

The Convention Council, meeting six months later, discussed some of the criticisms of Redpath's address that had come from various sources, including leaders of the Inter-Varsity Fellowship (later the Universities and Colleges Christian Fellowship, UCCF) and from some other Keswick speakers. The views of Stott and Redpath were discussed and it was generally agreed there was a *legitimate place on the Keswick platform for both points of view, provided they were not pre-*

*sented dogmatically.* Discussion continued over the next year or so. George Duncan, who was well known for his local church ministries (especially at St. George's Tron, Glasgow) and was the foremost Keswick speaker in this period, expressed his concern that, as he put it, "Keswick might lose its distinctive note and become a mere Bible Conference." To an extent Duncan's fears were fulfilled. Gradually the traditional Keswick teaching about how to receive the power of the indwelling Christ for victory over sin, as expounded by Keswick's early leaders such as Handley Moule, became less distinct. But a statement by the Convention's Council (produced in 2000 for the new millennium) about Keswick's position reaffirmed that the Convention was intended to encourage submission to the Lordship of Christ in personal and corporate living, and also to encourage "a dependency upon the indwelling and fullness of the Holy Spirit for life transformation and effective living."

---

A stress on the person and work of the Holy Spirit, especially on the filling of the Spirit, was characteristic of Keswick from its beginnings, but in the 1960s the Convention had to respond to the emerging charismatic movement, with its introduction of an expectation of a baptism of the Holy Spirit as an experience subsequent to conversion and associated with *gifts* of the Spirit such as speaking in tongues. In 1963, a year when eight thousand people were reckoned to be at the Convention, a clear reference to the charismatic movement was made by Herbert Cragg, who had an influential ministry at Christ Church, Beckenham, Kent. Cragg said that he had recently been asked if he had the gifts of prophecy, of healing and of tongues. The timing suggests a link with what was taking place at another of the Beckenham Anglican churches, St. Paul's, where the vicar, George Forester, and some of his parishioners were in that year seeking the baptism of the Spirit and the gift of tongues. This was also the year that Michael Harper, a curate at All Souls, Langham Place, claimed to have received the baptism of the Spirit. Responding to these developments, another Keswick speaker, Leith Samuel, minister of Above Bar Church, Southampton, stated that the key to holiness and power was not through speaking in tongues; it was through surrender to the Lordship of Christ. In this he echoed the message of a dominant Keswick speaker earlier in the twentieth century, Graham Scroggie, who had opposed the Pentecostal teaching of his period. By the mid-1960s the subject of the Holy Spirit with His gifts was becoming a major talking-point in evangelicalism. Keswick was, in this period, to take a cautious position.

At the 1964 Convention, John Stott's new book *Baptism and Fullness*, on the work of the Holy Spirit—a book that argued against a post-conversion experience of the baptism of the Spirit—was recommended by A. T. Houghton. The authority of Tim Houghton as a Keswick spokesman was indisputable, resting as it did on his position as Convention Council chairman, his distinguished missionary service, and his appearance as a speaker at twenty-three Conventions from 1942 to 1974. Maurice Wood, also a regular Keswick speaker, similarly recommended Stott's booklet, as well as Scroggie's approach to the baptism of the Spirit. Wood's advice to his listeners was to concentrate on *practical* holiness. Michael

Green, an Anglican theologian and evangelist who was to be associated with charismatic renewal, was also a Keswick speaker in 1964. He argued that Pentecost was unique and that the filling of the Spirit was not a "second blessing," although he did quote F. B. Meyer on desiring to be filled with the Spirit. For Leith Samuel, speaking in tongues was certainly not a sign of the baptism of the Spirit. He warned, in words reminiscent of Scroggie's approach over Pentecostalism, that if a person's experience went against Scripture it was so much the worse for that person's experience. It was noted in a Council meeting in 1965 that "letters had been received suggesting that there were anti-Pentecostal remarks contained in more than one [Convention] address." In 1966 Leith Samuel returned to the subject, seeing the times as characterized by confused teaching. There was, he suggested, a danger of *cults of the Holy Spirit*. He argued that the evidence of the fullness of the Spirit was not unusual temporary experiences but a *continued increase in Christ-likeness*.

There were, however, conciliatory voices to be heard at Keswick. Maurice Wood, the Principal of Oak Hill Theological College, was concerned about division over tongues and did not want to see polarization. The Spirit, he urged, is to make us *one*. Alan Redpath highlighted the work of the Holy Spirit and drew attention to 1 Corinthians chapter 12 with its teaching on the Spirit's gifts. In 1975 John Stott spoke at Keswick of the possibility of a subsidiary gift of prophecy in the exposition of Scripture, exhortation, encouragement and consolation, but he ruled out the contemporary ministry of prophets such as those in the New Testament. In part the difficulties may have been due to misunderstandings on both sides. When David Watson, an Anglican clergyman who became known for his ground-breaking ministry at St. Michael-le-Belfrey, York, and his wider evangelistic work, entered into an experience of the fullness of the Spirit he came to a new understanding of spirituality. "Spiritual life," as he now saw it, and as he commented on it, "was not to be entered into by an intensification of dedication," as Keswick seemed to teach. In fact Watson's view of the fullness of the Spirit was very close to the original Keswick position. The Spirit's fullness, for Keswick, was first and foremost a *gift of God*, not a matter of intensified dedication. In 1982 the Keswick Council expressed their unease about a booklet by David Watson on the Holy Spirit being commended at the Convention. No leader within charismatic renewal was invited to speak at Keswick until the 1990s.

By 1993, however, Philip Hacking, looking back over nine years as chairman of Keswick and over his decades of Convention involvement (he first spoke at the Convention in 1963), said: "I have been ministering at Keswick during the days when the charismatic movement has been at work in our land. That ministry has had both its blessings and its problems. It has been a joy to me to see some movement of unity between classic evangelicals and those who are charismatic, on things which are central." Philip Hacking had been in favor of David Watson being invited to speak at Keswick, but at the time this suggestion had not been acceptable. The more open policy advocated by Hacking was, however increasingly pursued. For example, from the mid-1980s various seminars were planned in different venues around the town and these encouraged greater active participation by Convention-goers. The seminars were either of topical interest or dealt with the particular theme of the week and were not necessarily directly related to the holiness agenda that dominated earlier Conventions. Further adaptation followed in the 1990s. As chairman, Jonathan Lamb, who had a Brethren background (most chairmen had been Anglican clergymen) spoke about the neglect of the person and work of the Holy Spirit, and suggested that the Wesleyan and Keswick traditions had been unusual in speaking of the ministry of the Spirit. Now, he noted, there were acres of books and miles of ministry cassettes on the Spirit. Lamb, although aware that there had been much division and bitterness, was thankful for this spiritual enrichment.

Discussion about issues connected with the Holy Spirit, as with issues regarding the meaning of being "dead to sin," occurred at a number of Convention planning meetings. Divisions between conservative evangelicals and moderate charismatics have become, however, less distinct today than they were in earlier decades. Among those at Keswick who have acted as bridge-builders have been successive ministers at Gold Hill Baptist Church in Chalfont St. Peter, Buckinghamshire, Jim Graham and Stephen Gaukroger. Both of those have been regarded as key influences on the moderate wing of the charismatic movement, and have been welcome speakers at Keswick at different times. The first ordained Pentecostal minister to join the Keswick Council was Joel Edwards, who shortly afterwards became general director of the Evangelical Alliance in Britain in succession to Clive Calver. He was attracted to Keswick primarily because of its holiness roots and his concern for that message to be heard more widely, though due to the weight of other responsibilities he reluctantly had to resign from the Council in 1999.

In short, after a period when Keswick seemed to be at odds with those who were newly taking up its own traditional emphasis on the Holy Spirit, the Convention has re-engaged with wider currents of thought within evangelicalism in relation to the Spirit.

---

With its motto "All One in Christ Jesus," the Convention operated from its beginnings as a stimulus to evangelical unity—spiritual, not ecclesiastical unity. Until the 1970s, Keswick was the best known and best attended gathering of Christians in the United Kingdom. Together with the mini-Keswicks held across the country and around the world, the Convention represented a powerful network. Gradually, however, other events not directly connected with Keswick emerged. In 1955 Lindsay Glegg set up the "Filey week" in the Butlins Holiday Camp on the Yorkshire coast, having first approached the Keswick Council to ask them to consider a second week at Keswick specifically geared towards helping the converts from Billy Graham's crusades in London and Glasgow in 1954 and 1955. The Convention considered the request but turned it down, so Lindsay Glegg went elsewhere. In fact, in 1969 the Council did start a second week at Keswick, which has grown to be equal in status and attendance to the first week, though for some years it was called the "Holiday Convention," with fewer meetings being arranged and more family-related activity. A third week began in 2001, which reflects the considerable success of week two in attracting families and younger people. The total number of individuals attending Keswick, over the combined three weeks, has reached 12,000.

In the 1970s and 1980s, however, it seemed that Keswick was in danger of becoming somewhat marginal to British evangelicalism compared to its previous central position. Certainly there were still very well known speakers at Keswick: Anglicans, including Kenneth Prior, Alex Motyer, Michael Baughan, Richard Bewes and Keith Weston, a Keswick chairman in this period; Baptists such as Alan Redpath, Stephen Olford, Raymond Brown and Francis Dixon; Church of Scotland ministers like George Duncan and Eric Alexander; and Methodists, most notably Donald English, who was twice President of the Methodist Conference.

But for some the Keswick platform was too conservative. In 1979 *Spring Harvest* was initiated as—at least to some extent—a young people's alternative to Keswick, sponsored by British Youth For Christ, which was then headed by Clive Calver and *Buzz* magazine, whose editor was Peter Meadows. These two pioneered Spring Harvest, initially in a holiday camp context in North Wales. In an interview in 1989, Clive Calver stated: "Pete Meadows and I started off . . . trying to begin an alternative to Keswick. And we *said* we did—not because we had anything against Keswick, but because we felt that *our generation* needed an expression of corporate spiritual life. . . . Spring Harvest did not start off as a charismatic event; it started off as being a teaching/training event. And its major thrust was young people." Younger people began to attend Spring Harvest in large numbers, with total attendance rising to 80,000 as it spread to other venues and other weeks. A measure of polarization began, with Keswick being seen by some as a retreat for older people.

Numbers attending student and youth meetings at Keswick began to dip, and grey hair among those in the main tent became increasingly in evidence. Some evangelicals from outside the Keswick constituency began to dismiss the Convention as no longer capable of making the same significant contribution to mainstream evangelicalism as it had done before.

The Keswick Council itself began to wonder if the Convention had in fact served its purpose and should end. On the human level, it was probably due to the sheer enthusiasm, stamina and determination of Philip Hacking, vicar of Christ Church, Fulwood, in Sheffield, and the chairman of the Convention Council in the 1980s and early 1990s, that the Convention not only did *not* die, but was *renewed* in vision and appeal. Philip Hacking put forward ambitious plans to build a permanent Convention center on Skiddaw Street in Keswick, which was opened in 1987. Alongside Philip was Maurice Rowlandson, the entrepreneurial director of the Billy Graham Evangelistic Association in Britain and a long-time friend of Keswick, who became Convention Secretary in 1979. The youth program at Keswick had diminished to a small group when Philip Hacking brought in Dave Fenton, his youth worker at Christ Church, Fulwood, to give fresh impetus to this area. Dave Fenton began to revitalize the youth work and, under the leadership of a skilled team, it became one of the exciting and growing dimensions of the Convention. The style of youth meetings has changed to include small group discussions as well as the major teaching input from the front and, more informally, the very popular *late night extra*. The Convention also teamed up with Spring Harvest and UCCF for a week in the Easter period entitled "Word Alive."

There have been many changes in worship styles within evangelical churches over the past four decades, and this has been reflected at Keswick. Tim Buckley from London Bible College (now the London School of Theology) put together a new chorus sheet in 1960, and in the 1960s also drilled a choir which sang the more familiar Keswick hymns. A new compilation of hymns, under the title *Keswick Praise*, was published in 1975, to coincide with the centenary of the Convention. With the start of the second Convention week in 1969, designed to cater for families with children, the style of worship—at least at "week two"—became more informal. A familiar pattern of worship at Keswick in the 1980s consisted of Tim Buckley leading from the platform, with a single musical instrument or perhaps two accompanying the singing. Use was also made of a brass-band ensemble playing in association with Ken Coates. In 1987 members of the All Souls Orchestra, conducted by Noel Tredinnick, were at Keswick for the special opening in that year of the new Convention building. The orchestra represented a rather dramatic change of style for Keswick. Some in the congregation felt that, in contrast with Buckley's fairly relaxed approach, they were being treated like the members of a choir. The music, too, was up-tempo in a way that startled at least one lady, who commented: "They've brought a jazz band to Keswick and I don't like it." More recently a small musical band to accompany the singing has been standard. Moves to incorporate the best of modern songs were led in the 1990s by Geoff Baker and John Risbridger. And in 1997 hymnbooks were replaced by closed-circuit TV screens.

The association of Keswick with wider evangelicalism

has been marked by the presence at Keswick of many leaders of the world evangelical community. A high point was in 1975 when, as part of the celebration of 100 years of the Convention, Billy Graham spoke at the Convention and at an open-air meeting in Keswick attended by over 15,000 people. Among the other well-known speakers in that year was Festo Kivengere, a powerful East African Anglican leader. Billy Graham's Convention address showed intimate knowledge of the Convention. He recognized that there had been internal disagreements in the past within the holiness movement and he insisted that Keswick had always stood for genuine Christian humility and had never taught sinless perfection. He quoted Graham Scroggie's contention that "the idea of sinless perfection would itself be a sin." But Graham also noted that on another occasion Scroggie had spoken a word of encouragement to those who had fallen away from their faith in Christ. For them, said Scroggie, there was a *gospel of recoverability*. The other points to which Billy Graham referred in this important message were Keswick's contribution to unity, the place of prayer in Keswick spirituality, the Convention's insistence on practical Bible teaching, its use of devotional literature, the emphasis on mission, and its expressions of social concern.

Graham's interpretation of early Conventions was that social concern was self-evident there. "Many of the audience of the early days," he pointed out, "came from country rectories or country houses; and in those days almost every rector's wife, and almost all the Christian ladies of the manor, looked after the poor and the old and the sick of the village. . . . Lack of social concern was unthinkable." Using the example of the leading Baptist among early Keswick speakers,

F. B. Meyer, Graham told his audience how Meyer rescued prisoners and found work for unemployed men. The call was for Keswick to be an evangelical witness that had significance in wider society.

———— —— —— ——

Often the message of change was presented at Keswick in individualistic terms, having to do only with personal holiness rather than the social issues raised by Billy Graham. With so many young people present at the Convention in the 1950s and 1960s—not least those at the InterVarsity Fellowship camps led by Arthur Pont and others—it was felt important that issues relating to living as a Christian in the world should be addressed. Dick Lucas, of St. Helen's Bishopsgate, London, speaking in 1964, contrasted the decade in which he was speaking with a period fifty years before, suggesting to the Convention that if dance halls were "filthy" then, they were far more so now. He made a similar point about the cinema, seeing it as a "disgusting institution." On the other hand, he warned that external taboos were insufficient to deal with the problems of living in the world. Such references point to the concern by evangelical leaders to protect their hearers from the sexual temptations they would meet in society. But wider social issues did not receive much attention at the Convention in the 1960s. A. T. Houghton, in 1966, speaking as chairman, made it clear that economic and social questions would not be addressed at Keswick. Its message was, he insisted, "full salvation." Nevertheless, it was hoped that the Biblical instruction given would supply answers to wider problems. These wider problems were soon to be addressed by a new generation of evangelicals with the formation of organizations such as TEAR Fund.

An American visitor, Paul Rees, giving the Bible Readings in 1967, was prepared to be bolder than Houghton. He touched on the race issue in America, mentioning Little Rock, Arkansas, which was associated with Martin Luther King and the fight for civil rights in the U.S.A. Rees continued: "You are looking at one minister this morning who is weary of hearing his evangelical brethren deal in the tactics of sneer and smear towards those we call 'liberals' because they are involved in the struggle for civil rights, racial desegregation, urban renewal and slum clearance, reduction of poverty and freer trade." He spoke of the way in which such Christians were dismissed as "social gospelers." Such criticisms, he asserted, "would go down far better if from our sound evangelical position we would exhibit a similar concern for the sheer human needs and problems and frustrations of the people around us." For a significant number of his hearers at the Convention at that time, however, the view taken of the social gospel was that it was a liberal invention which was in opposition to the evangelical message of individual salvation.

As an example of the way in which more recent Conventions have stimulated thinking about social needs, Stella Heath, of Torch Trust for the Blind, was challenged at Keswick's World Vision meeting in 1988. She was in charge of a group of visually impaired people at the Convention, part of a regular Keswick house-party organized by Torch Trust. Quite unexpectedly, during a song, she felt that God was leading her to go abroad and to find out about the situation of some of those who were visually impaired in the non-Western world. As a result, she spent five weeks in Zimbabwe, Zambia and Malawi. She discovered the desperate need of visually impaired people, who were often deprived of education and of the Scriptures in Braille. From the time of that visit, events moved with remarkable speed. Among the most significant ventures has been the setting up of a center in Blantyre, in Malawi, which has three houses for the visually impaired people of the region. One of these houses has been designated a Braille-production unit. The Convention's concern for world mission is being expressed in holistic ways.

There has been a greater emphasis since the 1990s on connecting the message of spiritual renewal with social involvement. Clive Calver, the director general of the British Evangelical Alliance (which saw huge growth under his leadership), speaking at Keswick in 1994, argued strongly for a recovery of evangelical social vision. For him "social action without the gospel is little more than sanctified humanism. But the gospel without social action is words without deeds; the two must go together." Two years later David Coffey, the general secretary of the Baptist Union and a Convention Council member, quoted from Graham Scroggie on the way in which the First World War had stimulated an adjustment of the old message to the new condition of things. Coffey suggested that Keswick would, in the 1990s, continue down the road of change. David Potter spoke at Convention seminars also, in 1996, on work with people with learning disabilities. In the following year there were daily celebrations for people with learning disabilities, run by Potter's own

Causeway organization. The Convention was also considering how it could contribute to work in the community of Keswick itself. Perhaps the earlier vision of a community-transforming spirituality, espoused particularly by F. B. Meyer, who was a leading social reformer, and by Stuart Holden, a Keswick chairman who was inspired in the early twentieth century by Meyer's vision, was being worked out in new ways.

Above all, in thinking about changes in society, evangelicals have prayed for spiritual revival and renewal. In his welcome to Convention-goers in 1986, Philip Hacking said: "We long for revival to come to our nation." He continued: "As I understand the message of the Keswick Convention it is basically that God, through His Word and Spirit, is still active in transforming power. If we look ahead to 1987 with eager anticipation for a renewed Keswick, as far as buildings are concerned, we must not wait until then for the renewal which we need right now."

Keswick has not been indifferent to the challenge of powerful renewal. Charles Price, later Principal of Capernwray Bible School and then senior pastor of the People's Church, Toronto, speaking at Keswick in 1990, referred to the Convention's more revivalistic past. Price, drawing from the Convention story, referred in one address to the revivals in Wales in 1904–5 and in East Anglia in the 1920s. He insisted that the message of the Convention could not simply be cerebral. For Charles Price there was contemporary relevance in the powerful 1922 Convention message by Douglas Brown (the chief evangelist in the East Anglican revival) warning against selective obedience to God. As Brown had done following his Bible Reading on that occasion, those present in 1990 were invited by Price to stand and to put things right in their lives. Philip Hacking spoke later of the very moving appeal that was made and the response to it. In the 1990s and in the new millennium Keswick's message has continued to give a central place to individual and corporate spiritual transformation.

———————

Keswick's concern for the world has involved a continuing commitment to world mission. The Missionary Morning, featuring many missionary testimonies, was moved from Friday to Wednesday, renamed World View, and later was moved again to the evening. The climax of that meeting has always been the closing appeal for people to respond publicly to God's call to Christian service at home or abroad, *at any place, at any time, and at any cost*. Many leaders in the Christian world look back on such an invitation at Keswick as a significant moment, including Philip Hacking and David Coffey, who in 2005 became the President of the Baptist World Alliance. The reason for the change to Wednesdays was primarily a practical one. Follow-up on site for those who had responded to the challenge had been limited, as Friday was the last day of the Convention. The whole approach changed with the arrival of the Christian Service Center (later renamed Christian Vocations), which brought enormous resources and practical skills to help people look ahead as they responded to the challenge of Christian ministry. This Midlands-based agency linked interested people with areas of need in Christian ministry both in Britain and overseas, and was founded by Rosemary Harris, then a member of the Keswick Council, formerly of the European Christian Mission.

Although the call to overseas mission did not appear to be given such prominence at the Convention in the later twentieth century as had been the case earlier, there were speakers who issued a powerful challenge. George Verwer, the founder and international director of Operation Mobilization (O.M.), by the 1980s a large-scale interdenominational and international missionary organization, brought a significant challenge to the Convention in 1980. As he reflected on the history of Keswick spirituality and its relationship to mission, Verwer argued that perfectionism, a focus of anxiety in Keswick's early story, was hardly the greatest problem for twentieth-century evangelical churches. Fixing on what he considered to be the crucial issues for the 1980s, Verwer issued an impassioned plea to preach holiness and the Lordship of Christ. Mike Fitton, one of those who heard Verwer, had attended the missionary meeting feeling that it had little relevance to him. But when Verwer spoke of the needs of the world, Fitton thought: "Why don't enough people go?" Mike Fitton and his future wife, Gilly (whom he met that year in the Tent at Keswick), both felt a call to mission. In 1993 Mike Fitton was badly injured during his work as a policeman and had to retire from the police force. The result was that he began a ministry with Crusaders in the north of England.

Other individual stories can be told. In 1998 the *New Christian Herald* featured the story of Raymond and Elspeth Bragg from Workington. During the 1994 Convention they had realized that God was calling them to full-time Christian service and were given advice at the Convention. Since then Raymond had become a local evangelist, working mainly in schools. Robin and Sarah Hay, another couple affected by the missionary challenge at the Convention, were, in 1998, training at a missionary college, Redcliffe College. The report in the *New Christian Herald* noted that they had felt the call to overseas mission separately, Robin at the 1989 Convention and Sarah at the 1991 Convention. In a way that was reminiscent of older approaches to the missionary imperative, Robin did not propose to Sarah until she was also called overseas. There had been indications that they should work in Nepal. Part of this story was conveyed at the Convention. The Hays had, by 1998, left their jobs—in management consultancy and personnel respectively—and intended to work with the International Nepal Fellowship using their professional skills. Whereas the earlier Keswick vision was strongly orientated to evangelistic work overseas, more recent stories suggested the variety of ways in which efforts aimed towards the evangelization of the world could be undertaken.

To an extent, the fact that Keswick has moved away in more recent years from convening a specific missionary meeting with numerous testimonies has reduced the opportunities for women to play a public role as speakers. On the other hand, the 1980s saw women being appointed to the Keswick Council and taking a more prominent role. Rosemary Harris was the first to be appointed, in 1985, followed by Helen Cooke and Elaine Duncan in 1988. Each of these had significant influence within the life of the Convention. In the autumn of 1998 the Keswick Council agreed unanimously in principle to reintroduce women to the speaker team in future Conventions. The decision arose, as the Council statement put it, "from a prayerful application of Biblical teaching as a whole, from creation through to the post-Pentecost new community of God's people." The statement noted the role that women have played in the story of the Convention and the way in which their responsibilities within Keswick had been increasing. The move towards greater participation of women in the Convention had, it was noted, *not been divisive, but a significant contribution to the event.* In 2000 and 2001 there were women speakers at the main Convention sessions: Anne Graham Lotz and Jill Briscoe. Keswick has committed itself to encouraging gifted teachers, whether male or female, and is affirming a role for women for which Hannah Pearsall Smith, Jessie Penn-Lewis and others, not least those who organized the missionary meetings, argued.

Earlier connections between Keswick and a number of the Faith Missions continued into the second half of the twentieth century, although to a lesser degree than before, and new connections were also made. From the 1960s Nick Carr of the Overseas Missionary Fellowship (previously the China Inland Mission) was a regular Keswick speaker. Dick and Rosemary Dowsett, also of O.M.F., ran student camps at the Convention and Dick became a Keswick speaker in the 1980s. He also joined the Keswick Council. There were continuing links with China itself. In 1980 Peter Conlan, who had been deeply affected by a missionary challenge issued at Keswick in the 1960s and subsequently joined Operation Mobilization, showed a number of slides of China at the Convention. He had been the first Westerner to speak to some leaders of the Chinese Church recently released from prison. During the conversations he had been asked by the

Chinese leaders about A. T. Houghton, who had been a missionary in Burma, and about Keswick. In that period there was still considerable repression of Chinese Christians. An O.M. leader, Peter Maiden, followed Jonathan Lamb as Keswick Council chairman, and Peter Maiden also succeeded George Verwer as O.M.'s international director. World mission was reemphasized through Peter Maiden's purposeful leadership.

———  ——  ——  —

In the early twentieth century Keswick had a remarkable international network, and although this network has changed in character it has remained important, with numerous conventions around the world—on every continent —which are modeled on Keswick. A considerable number of Keswick representatives have continued to travel and speak in many parts of the world in the later twentieth century and early twenty-first century. For example, Singapore, the Philippines and Egypt were among the places to which Keswick speakers traveled in 1972. George Duncan, whose parents had been missionaries, was the Keswick speaker in this period who was most comfortable with an international role. Duncan spoke in 1975 of the variety that existed in conventions associated with Keswick, from the massive Maramon Convention at Kerala, South India, where numbers could rise above 100,000, to much smaller conventions, such as that in Hokkaido, Japan. In the Cayman Islands, out of a population of about 20,000, the Keswick meetings, which began in the later part of the twentieth century, attracted up to 500 people. Three "Keswicks" began in parts of Trinidad in the 1970s and 1980s. In the late 1990s the Barbados Keswick Convention in the Caribbean, held each February, was giving its speakers an outline very much akin to the outline at Keswick itself in the 1950s. Perhaps Australia has more "Keswick" conventions per head of the population than any other country, with gatherings in or near all the main cities. The significance of these gatherings has continued, and the Northern Territories capital of Darwin began a Keswick Convention in the 1990s. Other more recently launched "Keswicks" include the Keswick Christian Life Convention in Nairobi, Kenya, and the Keswick Convention in Romania.

Often conventions in other countries have wished not only to use the name "Keswick," but to draw Keswick speakers from Britain and America. A delegation of Japanese evangelical leaders attended Keswick in England in the summer of 1962, and received the warm consent of the then-chairman A. T. Houghton to use the name "Keswick" for the convention in Japan. Speakers were imported each year. Paul Rees of the U.S.A. was the most frequent speaker (22 times between 1962 and 1990), and George Duncan was a repeated visitor between 1963 and 1991. Other speakers from America and Britain who have often been invited include Alan Redpath, Stephen Olford, Philip Hacking, Keith Weston, Dick Lucas, Stuart Briscoe, and, in the 1990s particularly, Raymond Brown, the former Principal of Spurgeon's College, London. Charles Price, as Principal of Capernwray Bible School, was a speaker at the Japanese conventions and at many other Keswicks around the world. The Tokyo convention was held initially in a large hotel, before moving to nearby Hakone, a beautiful mountainous area very similar to the English Lake District. Other Japanese conventions followed and they now take place in eight locations, from Sapporo on the island of Hokkaido in the north to the island of Okinawa in the south. 1991 the Kyushu Keswick Convention commenced and in 1993 a convention was set up on Okinawa, a Japanese island of one and a quarter million inhabitants, south of the Japanese mainland. Each of the eight conventions has its own committee, but there is also a Central Keswick Committee which meets twice each year. Carefully prepared papers are presented, covering studies on the history of the movement, its distinctive features, the content and emphases of the messages and the spiritual qualifications of the speakers. An older Keswick approach is evident.

The themes that determined the progression of teaching at Keswick became the distinguishing characteristics of the many conventions around the world. One of the oldest gatherings outside of Keswick itself is the Belgrave Heights Convention held in the Dandenong Hills overlooking the city of Melbourne in Australia. At a time in the 1990s when Keswick itself was moving away from the language about its purpose that had been used in the Convention's earlier history, the Belgrave Heights Convention still used the older terminology. Speakers were told that the object of the ministry was "the cultivation and growth of the spiritual life in Christ as we find it in the Scriptures. . . . This involves the call to obey Christ as Lord . . . a godly lifestyle through the empowering and fullness of the Holy Spirit." The method used was that "the Bible is expounded and practical life application is made by speakers . . . there is a clarity and definiteness in the ministry speakers bring from the Scriptures as they deal with issues and encourage people to respond to God's Word." The ministry content was specified as standing "in the heritage of the Keswick Convention movement: 1) The reality and nature of sin and its devastating consequences; 2) The work of Christ on the Cross; 3) The Victory of Christ's resurrection and the power of Christ's resurrection life in the daily experience of the Christian; 4) The call to full surrender to Christ as Lord as living sacrifices; 5) The Presence, Power and Fullness of the indwelling of the Holy Spirit . . . revealing godly character [fruit] and enabling service and ministry [gifts]; 6) The call and privilege of witness and service in gospel ministry for Christ in Australia and overseas." Speakers were asked to expound Biblical passages "which particularly address these areas. In the light of the current church climate, we would like to see the issue of the Work of the Holy Spirit clearly and specifically addressed."

Although Belgrave Heights is an example of a convention which has retained the older Keswick approach to a remarkable degree, with other conventions there have been variations on the central themes of Keswick. For instance, all the meetings at America's Keswick were to follow the daily Keswick themes, but the evening sessions were termed "Victorious Life Hours," and were given a revivalist atmosphere. They were the responsibility of The Victorious Life Conference Division of America's Keswick. In the 1970s speakers at America's Keswick were given seven themes for the week-long conferences that took place throughout the summer in Whiting, New Jersey.* The link with the pattern at Keswick

---

*The Victorious Life Testimony, which ultimately became America's Keswick, initially operated out of an office in Philadelphia, Pa., and utilized the rented facilities of Princeton (N.J.) Seminary for its meetings. In 1920 the conferences were moved to the campus of Stony Creek School, Long Island, N.Y.

in England was obvious, but these meetings had their own particular variations, emphasis and vocabulary. Taken from a fairly lengthy brief issued to each speaker, they included the following seven points. The themes, to be developed over seven days, were: Awareness of need, God's provision for our need, Identification and union with Christ in His death, Absolute surrender, Submission followed by commission, Appropriation by faith of all that is ours by Christ, and The Lord's return. The evangelistic emphasis and the inclusion of teaching on the Second Coming reflect adaptation to the local context. In New Jersey a nine-day youth conference was also arranged, and speakers there were given the same recipe for the week, with the proviso that the two extra days provided "an opportunity to expand on these themes—treating identification in His death and union in His life as separate studies, and dealing more extensively with the continuance in the Christian life."

---

At Keswick itself, the twenty years since the mid-1980s have been marked by many significant changes, perhaps more changes than at any other time in the Convention's history. Some of the changes have had to do with property. The Convention owned two sites in Keswick, on Skiddaw Street, where the main Convention tent was erected each year, and on Eskin Street, where there was a second tent. There was

---

Not until 1924 did it find a permanent home on the spacious, lake-fringed grounds of the Colony of Mercy, a God-blessed ministry to men with various addictions, located in the "pine-barrens" of central New Jersey.

also a Convention Lodge on Eskin Street. All the facilities used by the Convention needed considerable renovation by the 1980s. There were discussions, as we have seen, about whether Keswick should come to an end, but after praying about and discussing all the issues the Convention Council took the view that the Keswick message, in particular the message of holiness, was still much needed within the churches. Under the chairmanship of Alan Neech and then of Philip Hacking, major moves were agreed upon and then implemented. The Skiddaw Street site was developed, with a two-story Conference Center being built to be used as a venue for smaller conferences throughout the year. This was opened in 1987. The cost of this was raised by the sale of the Eskin Street site, the Lodge, and a hall in Eastbourne that had been given to the Convention. Many donations were also received from individuals to enable this new vision to be fulfilled.

Along with the change of the physical environment from the late 1980s, changes in style also took place. At each of the evening meetings there was now one speaker instead of the traditional two speakers. With specific passages of Scripture being assigned to speakers for the main Convention meetings at Keswick there was systematic exposition of one particular book or section of Scripture by different speakers through the week, a practice already in operation at Spring Harvest. Keswick has also become a family event, with a high-quality program of teaching and ministry for all ages. The children's work has been led by Andrew and Alison Bradley and Colin Draper and a Scripture Union team; the youth work has continued to be led by Dave Fenton. The number of children and teenagers has been increasing each year over the past decade or more, as has the team of leaders. The most recent development has been a young adults "K2 stream" in week two of the Convention. Other new developments include the "Keswick Lecture" delivered each year. Jonathan Lamb, the chairman from 1996, inaugurated this lecture. Someone who is expert and known in his or her field is invited to present a lecture, usually relating to issues of national concern, though sometimes the topic is of specifically theological interest. Sometimes the lecturer may be a member of the speaking team for that year who is particularly qualified to contribute, but at other times a speaker is brought in especially for that one event. Another change is the demand by Convention-goers for cassette and video recordings—which are now ready within a few minutes at the end of Convention messages.

Administrative developments have continued. In 1997 the Rawnsley Hall, near the center of Keswick, was purchased. Formerly part of Keswick School, it came on the market when the school moved a little further out of town. The then secretary to the Council and general director of the Convention, David Gray, who was appointed to succeed Maurice Rowlandson in 1992, had a vision for Rawnsley Hall as a secured venue for the youth program of the Convention and also as a public hall available for use on other occasions by the wider public. This has now become a reality, but it is too small, so an additional tent is pitched on the grounds of Rawnsley Hall in order to accommodate both the children's work and the youth program on the same site. There has been some uncertainty as to whether or not the Convention administration should be primarily based in Keswick itself. During the time when Mark Smith had responsibility for this work, an office was established in Uckfield alongside the office at the Skiddaw Street Center. However, the current administrative work, led by David Bradley, is based in Keswick. Much effort has been invested into seeking to establish good relationships with the town of Keswick.

In the twenty-first century, how does Keswick see its role? Out of discussions within the Convention Council a statement was produced for the beginning years of the new century that addressed that question. "The Convention," said the statement, "is committed to the deepening of spiritual life in individuals and church communities, through the careful exposition and application of Scripture." The following specific goals were set out:

- to encourage submission to the Lordship of Christ in personal and corporate living;
- to encourage a dependency upon the indwelling and fullness of the Holy Spirit for life transformation and effective living;
- to provoke a strong commitment to the breadth of evangelism and mission in the British Isles and worldwide;
- to stimulate the discipling and training of people of all ages in godliness, service and sacrificial living;
- to provide a practical demonstration of evangelical unity.

Crucially, in terms of the history of the Convention, additional notes explained that the Convention wished to "ensure Christocentricity, with the Scriptures as the means of achieving this." The Convention was seen as "sustaining its emphasis on life-transformation, on an encounter with God, on the balance of cerebral and experiential, mind and will, Word and Spirit." This meant "a sustained commitment to preaching for conviction." Under the heading of life transformation, the Convention would "sustain the traditional theme of the Convention in relation to holiness, ensuring that this is directly relevant to the challenges of contemporary life." This contemporary theme was reinforced in the notes about emphasizing evangelism and discipleship. Finally, on the question of unity, the Convention wished to "occupy the evangelical center ground." It was noted that many events were becoming sectionalized and the desire at Keswick was that the Convention would genuinely sustain a breadth of involvement with evangelicals and an appropriate diversity in its speakers, music and programs. The spirit of this statement was inclusive, warmly welcoming all evangelical "tribes" and seeking, as it said, to operate "*with a generosity of spirit in this regard and no narrowing of our position.*"

The Convention's motto remains "All One in Christ Jesus."

*Ian Randall*

Note: Much of this chapter has been adapted from *Transforming Keswick* by Charles Price and Ian M. Randall (Carlisle, U.K.: O.M./Paternoster, 2000).

# Appendix

## Current Structure of Keswick Ministries

### Administration

Keswick Ministries is the working title of the Keswick Convention Trust (the Trust). It reflects the growth of the wider Christian ministry of the Convention which takes place throughout the year and around the world.

Keswick Ministries' slogan is "Bringing the Word Alive," which summarizes the Biblical core of its activity. In January 2000 the trustees adopted a Position Statement—which can be found on the website (www.keswickministries.org)—as an up-to-date expression of the aims and objectives of the organization.

In addition to the annual Convention weeks in Keswick (now expanded to three weeks), Keswick Ministries is advancing its purposes through a range of initiatives. These include the development of a literature program, with books of Bible expositions published as Study Guides, and plans for a new range of titles reflecting Keswick values. Then there is the continuing growth of other media, including audio and video/DVD resources, and the development of the website. Keswick Ministries is also taking an active interest in the development of other Keswick programs in the U.K. and around the world, and exploring how best to provide resources and training for youth leaders and also for emerging preachers.

In English law the Trust remains a registered charity and private company limited by guarantee. Its constitution allows for between ten and twenty-one trustees, who are men and women drawn from positions of leadership within the Christian church and parachurch organizations as well as those with business and management skills. Each trustee is elected for a term of three years duration, and he or she may offer himself for re-election on rotation until the age of 70 years.

The positions of Chairman, Vice-Chairmen and Treasurer are honorary and the General Director serves as Secretary to the Trust.

There are two other trading companies which relate to ancillary projects on the Rawnsley Hall site and Crosthwaite campsite.

## Property and Finances

Keswick Convention Trust owns two sites in Keswick, at Skiddaw Street and Rawnsley Hall on the edge of Main Street.

Rawnsley Hall is the former site of Keswick School. During the Convention it houses the children and youth activities as well as the Earthworks missionary exhibition. During the remainder of the year three charities rent the main property from the Trust, along with a year-round car park on the site for use by both local residents and visitors to the town.

The Trust holds a small amount of reserves.

The Activities of Keswick Ministries are funded by donations made at the annual Convention and by a growing number of committed contributors (Keswick Partners) who make regular payments throughout the year.

The incoming funds are spent on tent installations and rental of equipment, accommodation, honoraria and travel expenses for speakers and volunteers, supplies and activities for the Convention, together with the ongoing ministry of Keswick Ministries throughout the year.

The Missionary Hospitality Fund makes grants to overseas Christian workers, which finances their holiday accommodation at the Convention. The Fund is supported by specific gifts and collections made at the Convention.

The work of Keswick Ministries is funded from general donations and other income streams, including royalties on book and tape sales, leasings, car park charges from the Rawnsley Hall site and rental income from the Convention Center. The residential accommodation in the Center, opened in 1987, is available on a rental basis throughout the year. Over the years, legacy income has also been a source of significant funds.

# Organization

The Keswick trustees take an active part in planning the Convention and carrying out specific roles and responsibilities during the event.

There are nine salaried staff members including the General Director, Director of Programming and Operations Manager. Five staff members are full-time and four work part-time for Keswick Ministries. Since the relocation of the office from Uckfield, East Sussex, in 2004 to Keswick, four staff have been appointed to work with two others already working there. The remaining three staff work from home elsewhere in the U.K.

In summary, the work of the General Director relates to the strategic development of the partnerships with Keswick Ministries' external contacts. There are nearly forty independent local "Convention" meetings in the U.K. and a growing number overseas (including the U.S.A. and Canada).

The Director of Programming works with a sub-committee of the Council to plan the teaching and seminar program of each Convention. His role also includes training courses, under the "Root 66" label, particularly aimed at supporting Keswick Ministries' flourishing work among young people.

The Operations Manager and his staff handle all the practical details of the Convention and on-going activities of general administration and finance.

The Keswick Council meets three times a year (including two consecutive days requiring an overnight stay) and has an annual prayer conference in May, in addition to the monthly prayer meetings, which are held in Keswick.

There are working groups and sub-committees which report to the Council and support its work: Mission Action Group, Program Committee, Logistics and Technical Committees and a Town Liaison Group.

For further information about Keswick Ministries and its work please visit the website or write to Keswick Ministries, Convention Centre, Skiddaw Street, Keswick, Cumbria, CA12 4BY, UK.

David Bradley
General Director, Keswick Ministries
2006

# List of Sources

*Manuscript Sources*

*Keswick Convention Archives* (correspondence and papers of various dates, mostly at Convention Lodge).
*Keswick Convention Minute Books:*
Trustees, 1901–16.
Council, 1917–
Mission Committee, 1892–96.
Mission Council, 1896–1917.
*Cowper-Temple Correspondence*, Broadlands Archives (letters mainly relating to the Broadlands Conferences and to the Pearsall Smiths).
*Diary of D. W. Whittle*, 1884 (at Northfield, Mass.).

*Printed Sources*
(probable date of undated books shown in brackets)

*Periodicals*

*The Christian.*
*The Christian's Pathway to Power.*
*The Life of Faith.*
*The Record.*
*Keswick Week*—1892 onwards. (1892, 1893 *The Story of Keswick*, and 1929–39 *The Keswick Convention*; 1917, 1940

omitted; 1941, 1944, *Keswick in Print*, 1942, 1943, *Keswick in London*).

## Books Primarily Concerned with Keswick

[1907] *The Keswick Convention*. Charles F. Harford, ed.
[1914] *Keswick From Within*. J. B. Figgis.
[1935] *These Sixty Years*. Walter B. Sloan.
1952 *So Great Salvation*. Steven Barabas.
1959 *Keswick's Authentic Voice*. Herbert F. Stevenson, ed.
1963 *Keswick's Triumphant Voice*. Herbert F. Stevenson, ed.
2000 *Transforming Keswick*. Charles Price and Ian M. Randall.

## Other Books

Braithwaite, R. *Life and Letters of William Pennefather*, 1878.
*Brighton Convention, The*, 1875.
Broomhall, Marshall, ed. *John Stuart Holden*, 1935.
Carré, E. G. *Praying Hyde* [1913].
*Dictionary of National Biography*.
Douglas, W. M. *Andrew Murray and His Message*, 1926.
Du Plessis, J. *The Life of Andrew Murray*, 1919.
Fraser, Agnes. *Donald M. Fraser*, 1934.
Fullerton, W. Y. *F. B. Meyer: A Biography* [1930].
Gairdner, W. H. T. *D. M. Thornton*, 1908.
Gammie, Alexander. *John McNeill* [1934].
Garrard, Mary. *Mrs. Penn-Lewis*, 1930.
Glegg, Lindsay. *Four Score and More*, 1962.
Hay, Archibald M. *Charles Inwood* [1930].
Hanbury, Charlotte. *Life of Mrs. Albert Head*, 1905.
*Canon Harford-Battersby and the Keswick Convention* by Two of His Sons, 1890.
Havergal, Maria. *Memorials of Frances Ridley Havergal*, 1880.

Hooker, Mary R. *Adventures of an Agnostic*, 1959.

Houghton, Frank. *Amy Carmichael of Dohnavur*, 1953.

Howard, Peter. *Frank Buchman's Secret*, 1961.

Jackson, Edna. *The Life that is Life Indeed: Remembrances of the Broadlands Conferences*, 1910.

Jones, R. B. *Rent Heavens*, 1930.

Langston, E. L. *Bishop Taylor Smith*, 1939.

Macbeath, Andrew. *W. H. Aldis*, 1949.

Macfarlane, Norman. *Scotland's Keswick* [1925].

Macgregor, W. C. *George H. C. Macgregor*, 1900.

Maclean, J. Kennedy. *Dr. Pierson and His Message*, 1911.

Mann, A. Chester. *F. B. Meyer*, 1929.

Millard, E. C. *What Hath God Wrought?*, 1891.

———. *The Same Lord*, 1893.

Morgan, Joy. *A Man of the Word*, 1951.

Nugent, Sophia. *Memorials of Charles Armstrong Fox* [1901].

Orr, J. Edwin. *The Second Evangelical Awakening*, 1949.

Padwick, Constance. *Temple Gairdner of Cairo*, 1930.

Page, I. E. *John Brash* [1912].

Parker, Robert A. *A Family of Friends*, 1959.

Pierson, D. L. *Arthur T. Pierson*, 1912.

Pollock, J. C. *A Cambridge Movement*, 1953.

———. *Moody Without Sankey*, 1963.

*Sister Eva of Friedenshort*, 1934.

Sitwell, Osbert. *The Scarlet Tree*, 1946.

Smellie, Alexander. *Evan Henry Hopkins*, 1920.

Smith, Hannah Pearsall. *The Christian's Secret of a Happy Life*, 1875, 1888.

———. *The Unselfishness of God*, 1904.

*Stevenson Arthur Blackwood*, 1896.

Stock, Eugene. *My Recollections*, 1909.

———. *History of the Church Missionary Society*, Vol. III, 1899.

Westbury-Jones, J. *Figgis of Brighton*, 1917.

# Index